GOD'S SEARCH FOR MAN

Sermons

BY KARL BARTH

FORMER PROFESSOR OF THEOLOGY IN THE
UNIVERSITY OF BONN, GERMANY

AND

EDUARD THURNEYSEN

MINISTER OF THE REFORMED CHURCH,
BASLE, SWITZERLAND

English Translation by

PROFESSOR GEORGE W. RICHARDS, D.D., LL.D., D.TH.
THEOLOGICAL SEMINARY OF THE REFORMED CHURCH
IN THE U. S. A., LANCASTER, PA.

REVEREND ELMER G. HOMRIGHAUSEN, S.T.M., TH.D.
MINISTER OF THE REFORMED CHURCH, INDIANAPOLIS, IND.
PROFESSOR-LECTURER IN BUTLER UNIVERSITY

PROFESSOR KARL J. ERNST, PH.D., D.D.
MISSION HOUSE THEOLOGICAL SEMINARY,
PLYMOUTH, WIS.

TRANSLATION READ AND APPROVED
BY KARL BARTH

EDINBURGH: T. & T. CLARK, 38 GEORGE STREET
1935

PRINTED IN THE UNITED STATES OF AMERICA BY
SELECT PRINTING COMPANY, INC., NEW YORK, N. Y.

PREFACE

IN ACCORDANCE with the wish of the publishers, this
volume contains a wide selection of sermons preached
by the Reverend Eduard Thurneysen, D.D., and Professor Karl Barth, D.D. They were selected for us
by Dr. Thurneysen from the various German publica-
tions in which they appeared. In arranging them we
have not considered any particular sequence whether
as to thought or author or text. A similar volume will
appear shortly in German.

Some of these sermons are simple, others more complex, but all of them have been preached to living
audiences. Some are of recent date, as the reader will
notice when he reads the first two. They all breathe
a vigorous faith born in a time of great social tension.

Needless to say, these sermons are expository. They
are based upon the fundamental fact that Christianity
originated in a living event. That event was not so
much a datum as it was a living tradition of force and
energy and faith. All preaching, as such, must remain
true to that original Word of God that gave it birth
and issued in the first Christian fellowship and its atti-
tudes of faith and hope and love.

v

It is significant that these sermons appear at the Lenten season. They lay great emphasis on the spirit of repentance which is for every man an essential experience in his approach to God and the channel by which God becomes great in and among us by sharing with us His grace and life.

None of these sermons argues about God. None seeks to establish a case for a peculiar theology. All bear witness powerfully to the mighty fact of God's self-revelation in Jesus Christ. From a firm faith in something done for them, these preachers proclaim to a confused and seeking world a God who is more eager to be our God than we are to be His children or our neighbor's brothers. Far from analyzing the situation, these sermons proclaim a centrum of victorious life that is not divorced from social implications but rather precedes social action and gives it that fulcral power which comes of setting life in eternal backgrounds.

These sermons are not offered to the reader in order to promote such a thing as Barthianism. It would be a travesty for anyone to read these sermons with a biased mind or in a partisan spirit. They are offered in the humble hope that they may lead us all to the Only One Who Matters. His Word is beyond our words and His Way must transcend and radically transform our petty human ways.

Lent, 1935.   E. G. H.

CONTENTS

GOD'S SEARCH FOR MAN

I.

THE GOOD SHEPHERD *

I.

I am the good shepherd: the good shepherd layeth down his life for the sheep. He that is an hireling, and not a shepherd, whose own the sheep are not, beholdeth the wolf coming, and leaveth the sheep, and fleeth, and the wolf snatcheth them, and scattereth them: he fleeth because he is an hireling and careth not for the sheep.—*John 10:11-13.*

Let us begin without delay with the decisive fact in our text. In what was read we did not hear someone speak *about* the Good Shepherd. We did hear someone call and interpret himself: I am the Good Shepherd. It would really not be worth our while to go investigating what books or our imagination or life claim to know about a good shepherd. We shall do better in attending only to Him who says of Himself: I am the Good Shepherd. We must seek to understand Him in order to gain from this vantage point a better understanding of what the parable of the Good Shepherd says. The parable could not verify Him if He did not verify the parable.

Who is speaking here? Jesus Christ! But who is Jesus Christ? Let us lay aside for a moment what we

---

* Sermon preached in the Evangelical Lutheran Christ Church in Paris. Part II follows on page 13.

I

think we know of Him and let us hear this answer: Jesus Christ is He who professes this "I am." Not only may He make it His profession without being guilty of mad arrogance; He must make it; for on His lips it is self-evident. Jesus Christ is He who verifies the parable of the Good Shepherd. He is what it signifies and what it could never signify without Him. Jesus Christ is He who is now and here in our very midst, with and in His word, our Good Shepherd. And all of us—believers and children of the world, the thoughtful and the superficial, the curious and the indifferent, the open-minded and the distrustful—He makes all what we are and what we could never make ourselves by our own selves as He makes us His people and the sheep of His pastures. This is Jesus Christ; even He who here and now meets us as our Lord when He says in His word: I am the Good Shepherd. Known or unknown to us, it is He who stands in the center of our life. We have been, long since been, told so in and with our baptism, and it will remain true to the end. It is He—again whether we know it or not— who marches as the Lord through the nations. In the very midst of every change and catastrophe of history He calls, gathers, rules, illumines and comforts His holy church, whose members—so He tells us today! —you and I are and shall eternally remain. But now let Him continue and interpret all that it means and signifies.

"*The good shepherd layeth down His life for the*

sheep." So He says. And we are further told that this constitutes the difference between the Good Shepherd and the hireling whose own the sheep are not and who therefore flees. When the hireling sees the wolf coming he leaves the sheep to their murderer. We are reminded here of the fact that we have not only a shepherd but also an enemy. As the sheep are powerless against the wolf, so we cannot defend ourselves against our adversary. Instinct may warn the sheep, but they do not really know what the wolf's presence means until he is upon them. But then it is too late. So it is with us and our foe. Let us not philosophize about him!

Let us, however, pay attention to the fact which is here presented to us: An enemy is threatening us. If we sum up our life in its totality—its good and evil days, its joys and sorrows, its springtime hopes and autumn disappointments, the power and success of men's mind and weakness and failures, the rise and fall of nations and civilizations—we may discover at its fringe, on the periphery of our life's totality, an abyss, a darkness, a last hazard. It jeopardizes our whole life. It is the final threat to which our whole life is exposed. Who thinks of this ultimate menace? None of us does! On our lonely mountain tops and in the crowded valleys of our life we have so many other things that challenge our interest. And to give thought to yonder enemy, we ought to know him.

We have, however, as little real knowledge of him

as the sheep has of the wolf until the wolf has come. When life's last peril has come it is too late, for it will be an enigma defying every answer we shall give. It will rise before us as an accusation against our whole life, and we shall have neither defense nor excuse to offer. It will be like a plunge into a yawning void and there will be nothing to stay or stop our precipitous fall; a torture it will be and nothing to relieve it. This is what threatens our life! Do we not sometimes become dimly aware of it? Do we not occasionally see it like a flash of lightning on the far horizon, on the periphery of our thoughts? In a terrifying dream? Even sometimes in moments of cool and sober reflection? The question disturbs us at times: What about my whole life? What about humanity, so colorful, so mysterious and mystifying? But we do not have a real knowledge of our foe. No, we do not have it! We could not escape thinking forever about it, and even the mere thought of it would consume us. But whether we give it thought or not, the final hazard to our life is there.

To be human means to have forfeited life. How do we know? We were told, "The Good Shepherd layeth down His life for the sheep." Verily, He does not lay down His life except for a very good reason. That menace became an event. And He, He suffered this event, and the event cost Him His life. We hear Him call and cry out: "My God, my God, why hast Thou forsaken me?" The deadly threat of life which imperils every man's life became here an event. He endured and suffered it. And hence we know that this danger exists. We have forfeited our life, even if we have no real knowledge of it; even if we refuse to give it serious thought. He, He ventured to meet this peril for us; and for us He perished in it. Thence we know the menace which puts our life in jeopardy.

And now let us hear that nothing and no one but the Good Shepherd will do this for us. No one delivers us from this final menace. Our text mentions an hireling who flees. At sight of the wolf he fails us. Who may the hireling be? Only one figure challenges our consideration here. But this figure appears in a great many disguises. It is man himself as he is his own master and guardian in every phase of his life and existence. See his strength! His wealth! His vitality! See his resourcefulness in fashioning and mastering life in ever loftier curves! See his success in ferreting out and utilizing the hidden mysteries of life! See his skill in discovering its beauties and in enjoying them! What burdens of grief and sorrow and despair can he endure! How well, aptly and cleverly he manages to hide himself from himself; yes, to run away from himself in the hour of his bitterest distress—by taking his own life! How well does he practice the even greater art of collapsing once, twice, thrice, only to rise heroically again and again until the hour of his final collapse arrives!

Shall we really not entrust ourselves to him as our Lord and guardian who is master of so many arts? Perhaps we merely fail to choose him because we are not aware of the real extent of his capacities, which reach from heavenly joy to mortal grief. Perhaps we ought to realize first how all-inclusive man's capacities are in order to understand what it means if we refuse to entrust ourselves into the hands of man. There is only one serious reason for not placing our trust in him: he will not guard us against the final menace of our life. He may be an excellent master and guardian in his sphere, but where life in its totality is at stake; when the enemy threatens us from beyond our life; when the abyss yawns; when we must plunge into the bottomless void; when life's final torture engulfs us—there, there he fails us. He refuses to take responsibility there. There he flees and leaves us alone with the terror from which there is no escape. "The hireling sees the wolf and forsakes the sheep and flees." Man is capable of many things. But in the end he proves to be a poor master of himself and a guardian faithless to himself. Have you never seen the terror, the perplexity and cowardice which make him surrender to the enemy when matters take a really serious turn? Have you never seen how helpless man is in the cruel hands of his adversary? Master and guardian, where are you now? But let not our judgment be too hard and harsh! The hireling's flight is partly excused, for he is only a hireling and not the shepherd whose the sheep are.

Man does not belong to himself. The man who is his own master is a poor substitute for his true Lord. We are therefore not in good keeping in his hands.

Under his rule everything may seem to prosper for a season, but when our total life is at stake it comes to the light of day what it means that man is not his own. For then man breaks faith with himself. O you rich and strong and vital man! You have many accomplishments! But this one thing you will never accomplish. You will never save yourself! When you fall into your most real and deepest misery—and everything else was perhaps never real misery—you cannot help yourself! No, he who is afraid of the last peril of his life will not entrust himself to you! He knows that he is not his own. He knows that in the hour of his last and greatest danger he will prove himself unreliable, untrustworthy, faithless! How do we know? Neither do we know this from ourselves, as little as we know of the final hazard of our life.

Left to ourselves, we would ever again believe that we are our own. Left to ourselves, we would live on in the imagination that we shall prosper in all circumstances and in all eternity. Left to ourselves, we would most probably trust and believe that we shall be and remain faithful to ourselves to the bitter end. But because we have the Good Shepherd, who does for us what we cannot do for ourselves—who layeth down His life for the sheep!—therefore and therefrom we know both that we are living under a constant threat and that we are not our own, and that the hireling offers poor protection.

But we have the good shepherd. He is the Good

Shepherd who layeth down his life for the sheep. In this manner He testifies and so He confirms that they are His sheep. The Good Shepherd is then He to whom we absolutely belong. Let us lay aside every useless objection to this large truth. His are also the lonely people who, humanly speaking, recognize neither outward nor inward bonds of fellowship. His are also the proud lovers of freedom who cannot endure the thought that they belong to another.

His are also all in whose philosophy of life the thought of the Good Shepherd plays no role. For as the final peril unasked jeopardizes every man's life, so we all belong unquestionably to Him who is greater than the final threat of our life. In the very face of this last threat, where it comes to the light of day that we are not our own, we become also aware whose we really are. Where we fail as masters and guardians of ourselves He intercedes for us and becomes active as our Lord and guardian.

But here also we must say that we cannot know and discover by ourselves that we have this Good Shepherd. Let us not be surprised if someone says "Such a figure has no place in my philosophy of life or in the world order in which I believe." How should it appear there? The Good Shepherd is the eternal mystery. It remained hidden from all ages and generations until it made itself known in the fulness of time. And the mystery will continue to remain a mystery to even the acutest and deepest thinkers unless it reveals itself; reveals itself in such a manner that it does not need to remain a mystery even to a little child; in such a manner that we all may simply proceed and really possess the Good Shepherd. Let it then be held forth for us what the Holy Scriptures tell us, what the church confesses and proclaims, what baptism and the Lord's Supper testify: Greater than the whole world, with its heights and depths, and greater even than the last peril is He who has created all and everything.

We have forgotten Him who is God. We did not obey Him! Therefore the last peril threatens us. This is what makes it so terrible and so dangerous. It is our guilt! Only our guilt! This is what severs us from Him. It is life in hell. But we are saved from this life which is really our due. For God saw the danger threatening us. He did not desire that we perish in it and be lost forever.

The peril was so great that He alone could avert it, and avert it only by taking it upon Himself, suffering and perishing in it. And so great was His love for us that He did this very thing. He veiled His deity and became man in His only begotten Son. And the last peril of human life came over Him: the misery of life without God; the penalty of sin. Death and hell's tortures did He suffer as they never came to any man. Thanks be to Him! And as He who is the Son of God and our Lord Jesus Christ perished in it, it lost its dangerous character. It can no longer close in upon us. His sufferings on the cross are the birth pangs of a new

and emancipated humanity which He brought to light
in His resurrection from the dead. He removed and
abolished the last hazard which imperils us and in which
we would perish. So He testified and proved indeed
that He is the Good Shepherd whose the sheep are.
This Shepherd was and remained faithful to us. This
Shepherd has done everything for us. He laid down
His life for us that we might have life.

This is good tidings! It is the mystery revealed! It
is the gospel of life! Praise God that we may deliver
and hear it! Praise God that it is more true than every
belief we hold of ourselves; true even beyond our
doubts and despair; true also beyond the sea of human
unbelief and half belief and misbelief and superstition
in the world and church! Praise God that provision is
made that the light of this message may shine in our
gloom; yea, that it outshines the multitude of artificial
lights with which we delude ourselves in our darkness.
We are not our own. We belong to Jesus Christ our
Lord. And this our Lord is our Saviour; our Comfort
and our Help. That we belong to Him is our salvation
in our last peril.

As we join in the hymn "Praise God!" there remains
for us a wholesome fear. It motivates all those to whom
it is revealed that they were saved before they knew
and understood the hazard of their life. He is in the
way to true wisdom and humility who lets himself be
told that this last peril threatened him, and that it does
no longer threaten him because God has made Himself

his refuge and his shelter. For us there remains only the law which is written on the tablets of every heart that has learned that we shall only disappoint, break faith with, and forsake ourselves at the critical moment.

He who has lost confidence in Himself will therefore receive guidance and instruction on the way he must go. His loss of self-confidence will teach him to run the course of the law and the ordinances of God. Liberty, true liberty, is the portion of him who is aware *"The Lord is my Shepherd, and the Good Shepherd layeth down His life for the sheep."* For all secret and public diffidence, anxiety, and subserviency have their origin in a want of assurance which is inevitable wherever a man thinks he must govern and protect himself. We shall lose them, lose them increasingly day by day, as day by day we see Him in whose hands we are. And finally ours is the task, the obligation, the high mission which lies inevitably on those who are aware of these things in behalf of those who do not yet know. For from unawareness come those misunderstandings where each will go his separate way. Thence come the hatreds and struggles of all against all, that we do no longer know—and always forget again—that we belong to the Son of God and that we have been saved by Him from the fall into the bottomless pit.

If we want to live we must ever be told anew; and every one of us is responsible that it is done. If the world is to live there must be a church which will tirelessly proclaim this message. It is our portion to join

the song of praise unto God!   But if we do it because
our eyes are opened for the miracle of mercy it is because we have received mercy.   It is a part of what God
the Father, our Lord Jesus Christ, and the Holy Spirit
have given to their own in incomprehensible sovereign
grace!

II.

THE GOOD SHEPHERD

2.

I am the good shepherd; and I know mine own, and mine own know me, even as the Father knoweth me, and I know the Father; and I lay down my life for the sheep. And other sheep I have, which are not of this fold: them also I must bring, and they shall hear my voice; and they shall become one flock, one shepherd.

—John 10:14-16.

The words which we have read form the second half of the gospel of the Sunday Misericordia Domini. On the first half, which speaks of the difference between the Good Shepherd and the hireling whose the sheep are not, I was privileged to speak last Sunday in the Evangelical Lutheran Christ Church in Paris before the Germans residing there, and many Frenchmen. Why should I not be permitted to continue with the text on this side of the Rhine at the opening of our Reformed convention before this purely German circle? Our eyes do not yet see the fulfilment of the prophecy with which our text closes: *They shall become one flock, one shepherd!* The Rhine—and not only the Rhine! —is much too deep. But if we heed this prophecy, spoken to us by the mouth of Him who is the truth, because He Himself *is* the Good Shepherd who is to come, we shall not wish to withdraw from the unity and fellowship of the word which is addressed without distinction to Germans and Frenchmen, Lutherans and Reformed.

Can we place our Reformed convention, can we place our common care of the church which has brought us together, under a better sign than by continuing in the gospel of Misericordia Domini, *i.e.*, of the Lord's mercy? For in this the church has her life and her nourishment, and in this she knows her every care well provided for in advance, that she may continue, simply continue, her text in the good tidings of the Lord's mercy.

When Reformed elders and ministers meet, as we do today, to counsel and determine in difficult times on the way of Christ's church on earth, it may comfort but also exhort and warn them that Jesus Christ says, I am the Good Shepherd. They may hold it as a shield before themselves and their weaknesses. But they must let it stand also as a strong bulwark against their own arrogance. See how this "I" stands there for and also against our "We"! We are the representatives and teachers of confessing, militant and suffering Reformed churches, Reformed according to the Word of God.

Well and good! We believe ourselves called and commanded to do what we are doing. We believe in our mission, and also in our justification and in God's blessing on our work. We have behind us many an encouraging and strengthening experience. We have the confidence and high expectation of thousands upon thousands in Germany and other lands. Surely we are conscious of living and working in a great and glorious period of the history of the church in spite of everything. In short, we have occasion to be thankful and to act with firm determination. But we are aware also that our situation is full of perils.

What do our few hundred Reformed churches in Germany signify in the midst of the current happenings in Germany? How many or how few of those who rule us today have taken even five minutes of their time to gain a sure knowledge of the nature and purpose of our Reformed faith? What can we do, or what may we hope to accomplish, in a realm in which professedly only one idea is to be valid and sovereign? And whatever may be our judgment on present-day affairs, surely this idea cannot be the one which must lie closest to our hearts! What can and shall we hope for in view of the fact that we ourselves are certainly not the united, courageous and faithful company which the present times demand? What may we expect in view of the deep uncertainty which is still, and becomes always again, apparent even in our innermost ranks? "We Reformed!" Oh, we have every reason to be filled with fear when we German Reformed men of 1934 look into each others' eyes. But over against our "We" His "I am the Good Shepherd" has been raised—by the Lord's mercy!—and it shall remain standing.

In these times and in the two days of our Reformed

convention we shall be and shall accomplish exactly as
much as this "I" rings in our ears as a word of valid
truth and duty.   External pressure shall not prevail
against this "I."   The might of men, be it ecclesiastical
or political force, shall not overcome it.   But neither
will our inner and most inward problem, the disharmony
between what we should be and what we are, vitiate it.
I am the Good Shepherd!   This word tells us that our
cause is not our cause.   Another bears and guides and
fights for it against every man who may attack and
scorn it.   And no less against us!   We need only to
watch faithfully His hands to be sure of our cause
whatever turn affairs may take.   But note well: against
this "I" our own insight, our good will and our Reformed self-consciousness must not seek to prevail
either.

Surely in a Reformed convention we cannot fold our
hands in our laps with the lame excuse of impotence.
We should be queer scholars of Calvin were we to do
this!   But in a Reformed convention it will not do either
to let political and ecclesiastical sagacity pry into the
mystery of the historical present and to seek to snatch
from it the greatest possible successes.   It is not our
business to help our own preconceived notions to a splendid success or even to save them.   Against that fine saying of Zwingli it cannot be *our* chief concern that *we*
should do some courageous and, if possible, victorious
deed.   *I* am the Good Shepherd!

He who would have the comfort of this word—and
we may and should have it!—must heed its warning

also. Nay, he must let himself be set right in the very bottom of his Christian conscience.

Unmistakably we are told that *we* are *not* good shepherds. Jesus Christ says, *I* am the Good Shepherd. It is part of the strange things in Roman Catholicism that it dares to apply this very gospel to Saint Peter, to the Pope, and to the church. As if this very gospel did not tell the church that she has a Lord—and is not called to exercise dominion! As if man—even the ecclesiastical or apostolic man—were not always the hireling who fails in the decisive moment! As if man belonged to himself and could therefore lead himself to good pastures!

If we who are here assembled are truly the church we shall hear this word: "I am the Good Shepherd!" All activity and all obedience, if it is real obedience, can come only from hearing it. But now let us listen a little more closely to what we are told. Are we the church? If so, we shall not have met without comfort nor without warning nor in vain.

In some form, perhaps in a very unexpected form, this Reformed convention will then be made to serve the glory of *God*, and therefore also the temporal and eternal welfare of His church on earth. But whether we are the church is not for us to decide. We cannot simply presuppose it, nor can we accomplish it by our own labors. Let us in this hour think seriously of the two forms of mischief which stand menacingly on the threshold wherever ecclesiastics meet.

Either men speak in a monstrous ecclesiastical self-assurance. They act as if *they* carried the Scriptures and the Confession and the Holy Spirit in their vest pockets and needed only to discuss their practical application. Or men speak in a nervous excitement. They think they must conjure the good Lord with all manner of incantations and arrangements for whatever program they may have prepared.

If we are a convention of either of these two types, we are certainly not the church. Over against this twofold mischief there stands in serious simplicity the only possibility for a real church convention. It hears the Good Shepherd say: "*I know mine own and am known of mine as the Father knoweth me and I know the Father. And I lay down my life for my sheep.*" This is the answer to the question if we are the church. It directs us to the threefold mystery of God. In honoring and adoring this threefold mystery as such we receive an answer to the question if we are the church and we are guarded against the twofold danger of all ecclesiasticism on earth.

Let us begin with the last: *I lay down my life for the sheep.* For this reason, and for this reason only, is there a church: because He has borne and carried away our guilt. Because God gave Himself for us in His Son. Because the Good Shepherd entered the peril of eternal death for His perplexed and helpless sheep and perished there. See, here they are met together: the terror that imperils us, and God's mercy which removes this terror. His mercy alone can do it and does it! Where this is known and kept in mind there is neither sordid self-assurance nor nervous excitability. There is the church.

And further: *I know mine own and mine own know me.* A mutual recognition between Jesus Christ and His own takes place. In this recognition, and in this alone and in no other reality, is the church constituted. The reality of the church is the light of the communion of the Holy Spirit. For this is the work of the Holy Spirit who is active in His sovereign goodness: that this mutual recognition comes to pass. The Good Shepherd discovers me and you in our lost condition and tells us: You are my sheep! And you and I discover the Good Shepherd, after having made so many other discoveries. And we say to Him: Thou art *my* Shepherd! Where this mutual recognition is known and where this sovereign goodness of the Holy Spirit is kept in mind, both as question and answer, there will most assuredly not be a convention of the self-assured nor of the nervously excited. No, there is the church.

And finally: *As the Father knoweth me and I know the Father!* In this manner, this mutual recognition comes to pass. It is the mystery of the love of the Father to His eternal Son and of the Son to the Father that there is for us the grace of our Lord Jesus Christ and the communion of the Holy Spirit. This divine mystery is the foundation and constitution of the church. Because within God himself, in the eternal mystery and majesty of His Godhead, takes place a fatherly and a filial recognition in a mutual love, therefore—therefore, then, be-

cause God is love within Himself—therefore the Good
Shepherd lays down His life for His sheep.

Therefore He knows His own and His own know
Him.   Here is the church—and how could there be
room for human self-assuredness or human nervous-
ness?—where one knows of this mystery of God as we
may know it since it has been revealed. If we are the
church, and not a convention of the self-assured and
nervous, we shall be saved from the temptation of great
and small ecclesiastical meetings of ancient and modern
times; namely, from the temptation of an orientation
secularly or politically sagacious and administratively or
tactically shrewd. As if there were other necessary and
urgent truths to be taken into consideration besides the
truth of the Triune God! The church has always suffered grievous injury, as she has also suffered in this
dark and stormy year of German church history, when
she yielded to this temptation—which offers so many
pleasant outlooks and enticements. Just so she merely
manifested that she has secretly ceased being the church.

Let a convention, a church meeting such as ours,
remain, abide and persevere—every individual par-
ticipant, in every concern, and in every vote he casts—
in that reverence and adoration of the threefold mystery
which constitutes the church. In the discussion of practical questions let it not degenerate into a parliament or
"leaders'" council! Let not the questions of what is
right and what duty demands become secondary to questions of practical success and expediency! Let it not
treat the Scriptures and the Confession as courts of last

appeal on the validity of which one first comes to an agreement only to play politics afterward on a foundation in which these courts of appeal are only ornamental and not fundamental! Let it be and remain a meeting of the church!

If our convention will do this, its deliberations will not remain without light, and its resolutions not without power. If it does not do so, it were indeed better we had never come together. Deliberations will then become vain talk and resolutions will be scraps of paper, no matter how profitable they may appear to be. But it will do this only if it *is* church even before. And the question whether she is church, God the Father, the Son and the Holy Spirit alone decide, according to our gospel. Let us examine ourselves, how our convention stands in the face of this question which is put to us. And let us call upon Him who alone determines here that He would not hide His face completely from us!

Finally, the words of the prophecy which form the end of the gospel: *"And other sheep I have, which are not of this fold: them also I must bring, and they shall hear my voice; and they shall become one flock, one shepherd."* Despise not prophesyings! There is good reason that a convention such as ours should keep this prophecy definitely in mind. In conformity with our peculiar origin and responsibility, in conformity with the peculiar service which the churches we represent desire to render, our convention is a Reformed convention.

We have reason not only to be not ashamed of our

Reformed confession and the form of our Reformed congregations but to be happy and proud of them. We have reason to be thankful that in this very year of temptations, struggles and sufferings, in spite of what may be laid to the charge of our Reformed people, our Calvin and our Heidelberg Catechism and our Psalms— or let us say it more simply and directly: our Reformed Scripture principle—have proved their worth. Unconsciously and indirectly they have done so also among many others who do not belong to our fold, and who would perhaps have it otherwise. We know again from life what for a long time we knew only from books— that with these weapons one can make a stand in all kinds of battles. Our convention must and shall stand under the sign of this gratitude, if God will. But— despise not prophesyings! This prophecy makes it necessary for us—and woe unto us if we are disobedient! —to look and think beyond the confines of our Reformed fellowship.

Neither the chief moderator of our Reformed Church nor the chief Elder of the Brethren nor the World-Bishop of the Lutherans is the Good Shepherd of our gospel. He is—mark the distinction!—King and Head of the church which is gathered in His Name alone. He has put us into the place we occupy without being Himself limited to our place. He has given us our task without exhausting His plans and purposes in our mission. He wants us to be faithful and upright Reformed men, but, "*Other sheep I have which are not of this fold; them also I must bring*"—not necessarily bring them to us but bring them to *Himself*—"*and they shall hear My voice.*" *My* voice, we are told, and not our voice, even if our voice be quite good and obedient, but the voice with which He will be pleased to speak to them and—they shall become one flock, one shepherd.

Today we cannot even fathom how it shall be. It cannot be our work to bring about this union. When He shall bring these other sheep and when they shall hear His voice, then this unity will come to pass. How can we fail to think of this unity now already at this our place and in the sign of our own mission? We may and must not look or think beyond the church into a world of thieves and robbers of which the beginning of this tenth chapter of John speaks, into the world of confusion and error and brute force, into the realms of Antichrist. We would not dare to call ourselves a Reformed convention were we to hesitate in the present situation in Germany, which is no longer complex but very simple and clear, to call light light and darkness darkness. We shall not and can not surrender to our evangelical brethren of another conviction our own convictions of faith and forms of doctrine and life well founded and which have proved themselves so well, especially this year. On the contrary, we shall insist on them without equivocation as a counterbalance, intensification and completion within the common evangelical confession.

Neither shall we forget what He says, where, to

friend or foe of the truth, we must say "No" or "Yes," but, *"Other sheep I have, and they shall become one flock, one shepherd."* Our Reformed convention must very definitely stand under the sign of this hope also. It will mean that we shall not have a self-willed and arbitrary understanding of our Reformed nature and purpose. What is there that would offer less occasion for self-will and arbitrariness than Reformed nature and purpose? Rather we must understand it as a service to the Lord and therefore in and for the evangelical church. Even in the form of those who have gone or have been led astray the church has a vague and even invisible existence, reaching deep into the camp of those to whom we must now, as to enemies, say definitely "No." It will mean that we shall not deny them our faithfulness, although we may be firm and even acrimonious. For the Good Shepherd will not deny them His faithfulness.

How much less shall we deny fellowship with those with whom we know ourselves one in the church in spite of serious divergences and differences in faith. To be faithful to each other, in hope even toward our enemies, means to remain together, to remain within earshot as long as a higher hand does not really separate us. To stay together because of the guidance and the voice of the Good Shepherd, who may want to make use of our service; under no condition refuse obedience in order to be available to Him unless He shall make an unmistakable demand for different action. Our deliberations may show us something of what it may mean in our concrete situation. But whatever they may show, we shall not follow any other watchword than the one to be present for Him and therefore also for the brethren, whether in unity as fellow partakers of their joy or as watchmen and warners in contentions and disputes with them—but present for them.

If it should please the Good Shepherd to bring forth out of the terrible chaos of the German Evangelical Church of today one flock, then the nature and purpose of our German Reformed Church shall certainly not bar the way. No, He shall find the Reformed men watchfully ready also in this direction, in regard to faithfulness to the brethren with whom we are one or not one. The Reformed congregations of those who would live of the Lord's mercy! The very mercy of the Lord drives us to hope. The representatives of these congregations will therefore counsel and resolve with the unequivocal petition: *"Thy* kingdom come!"

III.

JESUS THE LORD

And straightway he constrained the disciples to enter into the boat, and to go before him unto the other side, till he should send the multitudes away. And after he had sent the multitudes away, he went up into the mountain apart to pray: and when even was come, he was there alone. But the boat was now in the midst of the sea, distressed by the waves; for the wind was contrary. And in the fourth watch of the night he came unto them, walking upon the sea. And when the disciples saw him walking on the sea, they were troubled, saying, It is a ghost; and they cried out for fear. But straightway Jesus spake unto them, saying, Be of good cheer; it is I; be not afraid. And Peter answered him and said, Lord, if it be thou, bid me come unto thee upon the waters. And he said, Come. And Peter went down from the boat, and walked upon the waters to come to Jesus. But when he saw the wind, he was afraid; and beginning to sink, he cried out, saying, Lord, save me. And immediately Jesus stretched forth his hand, and took hold of him, and saith unto him, "O thou of little faith, wherefore didst thou doubt?" And when they were gone up into the boat, the wind ceased. And they that were in the boat worshipped him, saying, Of a truth thou art the Son of God.—*Matthew 14:22-33*.

We have listened to an Easter story which took place before Easter. The same large and incomprehensible light which bursts forth so triumphantly at the end of Jesus' life at his death and resurrection shines here also. The Easter event permeates the entire life of Jesus, even before the days of Easter. On Easter morning we stand in the full blaze of what always was in Jesus and of what was the mainspring of His life. Here at the empty grave and in the incomprehensible meetings of the Risen One with His disciples we have a final confirmation that Resurrection is the secret of His life. Here it becomes indubitably clear who He really is, this Jesus of Nazareth who died in deepest humiliation on Good Friday: the Son of the Father, He who comes from above and enters our dark world to link it up anew with the world of God. In the resurrection, in the momentous event in history which we call the "Life of Jesus," power from on high breaks forth and light from heaven bursts upon our night. They would prevail again in our world.

Power from on high! Light from heaven! The living God! Our story tells us of them. Of God who doeth wondrous things; of God who raises the dead!

In a stormy night, Jesus comes walking to His disciples over the waves. Whatever you may think of the story, it clearly tells us that around Jesus, the real Jesus, the Jesus of the New Testament, unheard of events become possible and real. Whoever comes near Him must be prepared to reckon with God's own might and power, a power lying far beyond every power known to us. In Jesus we see a dazzling flash of a new and unknown nature breaking through what we call nature. Jesus lives from energies of a world which are not of our world. He discovers and brings with Him an activity which will not fit into our systems. He is the fulcrum of events for which our history has no place.

Here in the very midst of history stands the end of all history. Here we are told, *"Heaven and earth and nature and history shall pass away!"* Even if at first sight we are tempted to lay the story aside as a pretty fable, even the pretty fable has a most remarkable meaning. It discloses a truth which makes all that we commonly call true thoroughly uncertain. *"I see a new heaven and a new earth!"* This is Jesus. It is the message of every story in the New Testament as well as of the Old. *"They bear witness of me"* applies to all the Scriptures. The whole Bible has no other content, in the last analysis, than to testify of Him who is coming from above. Its only purpose is to spell and speak out the name JESUS, in order to tell us, in and with His name, of GOD. But the God of the Bible is not the puny little godlet which men fashion for themselves with their concepts. No; He is the true and real God, the God who IS God, the God who doeth wondrous things. And Easter gathers all this together in one word of triumph and victory—Resurrection, Jesus' resurrection from the dead! In simple words, the Bible proclaims and explains the word "God" in such a manner that it becomes in the end that singularly strong and uniquely true word which it really is.

A momentous event takes place in us when we begin to become aware of the tremendous import of the word "God" in the Bible. Perhaps we try to evade it at first. We actually say that what we are here told of God are myths and fables. Doubts and trials assail us. This question bothers us: "This is God? Is He really so great, so important, so living, so near? Can one, nay, must one, really put his trust so blindly in Him that waves and billows mean nothing if only He is with us?" We cannot fathom it. It seems impossible, fantastically impossible.

We may feel like the disciples in that night on the lake—afraid to reckon with such a God. It is for us indeed like a leap into uncertainty, a foolhardy venture contrary to all reason. Surely we have a little understanding now for the desperate expectation in Peter's breast when he left his ship and stepped out on the water.

We are not easily led to leave our ships. But, on the other hand, is there not within us something that has long waited to hear of a strong and living God? Are we not tired, tired unto death, to be told of a God, and to pray to a God, whom we may and must not wholly trust? We are a remarkable lot. We do not easily leave behind us our doubts and scruples, and yet we would be rid of them. We yearn for the day that will make an end of twilight that is neither day nor night.

A radical daring keeps stirring in every human breast. There is a spark in every soul—perhaps it is only a spark, but a spark it is—that fires our joy in these power stories of the Bible. We feel that night is past here and a new and glorious day has come. Would we really have another Saviour than one who walks on the waters? A Jesus who failed to rise from the dead avails us nothing. What other reason is there for bringing us to church again and again? Were we to hear only of a God who, fortunately for him, measures up to our rule and who is able to do what we can also do ourselves without Him, what need have we of such a god?

Whenever the church has told men of such a tiresome little god it has grown empty. If the church offers only a little philosophy, a little morality, a bit of civic virtue even, or religious edification, we can dispense with her. We can get them in other places equally well, if not better. Why not turn on the radio or read a good book at home? But that radical daring, our yearning for the living God, will not be gainsaid. It lives when and wherever the church discovers the Bible. Men's souls will then come into their own. But the church must really discover it! Oh that it were given the church really to understand her misery and her grandeur! To understand that men really do hunger and thirst for the truth of the Bible because they yearn to break through the whole array of our gods into the presence of the true and living God! Then the church would be transformed. From a place half tedious and half solemn, which it is so largely, it would become today a place where men are roused and become fully awake; yea, it would be changed into a living fountain to quench the thirst of our age.

In Peter we meet with such radical daring. He reached out for the living God. What was it? Is it a trait of character peculiar to him? Is he alone blessed thus? Was he perhaps more resolute? Was he a genius? Or perhaps more pious than others? Certainly none of these things! We are told enough of him to know that he was as weak a man as we are. He did not even have a real conception of God and God's work. His ideas of his master Jesus were altogether wrong. A day even came when he passed through a most tragic collapse. But notwithstanding all his perversities, there were in him a hunger and thirst for the living God. And God had respect unto it and could make use of it.

As early as this hour, on the Sea of Galilee, long before his actual call to be an apostle of Jesus Christ, we see a flash of it. On one side he saw the turbulent waves and the black darkness of night. On the other he saw Jesus walking over the waters. And then he saw— and this is really decisive—that he cannot and must not remain standing still here. Timidity, indecision and irresoluteness are out of place here. Either—or! In that moment he understood something. He understood Jesus. Jesus!—and He is not some one, not even the highest and best of men. Jesus!—He is the One besides whom there is no other. Jesus, the Son of the Father! God's power! God's light coming to meet us in our dark and dreary world! He understood Jesus! With Him a crisis has come and all things shall become new. To understand this means to understand God.

If you have understood and do not now hesitate, God

can enter in and do something. A question flashes up before us. Is God Master and Lord or not? Does He care for us or not? Dare we continue to fear? To doubt? To mourn? Such questions Peter was compelled to answer. We also must make answer to similar questions as we look on the Jesus of our story. Because Peter understood Jesus, he knew also what must needs follow as his answer. He reached out and laid hold.

To stand before Jesus and to see Him does not mean to have a notion in the head or a sentiment in the heart. It does not mean to have noble thoughts or pious feelings. No, it means to lay hold on the truth and to let what is true become valid truth, but it is true only as it becomes valid truth. It is to become truth, valid truth, also in my life that God is mighty to save when storms rage and billows roar.

Is it really true? Does such help *come*, and come from God? If it is true that God's help is waiting to meet us, we cannot wait for help to come by itself, from men or from some unknown somewhere in or behind nature. We cannot, because Jesus is here. Jesus means: Help is come from *God*. Because this is true we can be helped. But we must suffer this help really to help us. We are in His hands. But we must now really commit ourselves into His hands.

When a man becomes aware of the living God; when he is called to make his decision in His presence; when he must commit himself really into God's hands, the day of the Lord has come for him. It is a never-to-be-

forgotten moment in life.   Let me point out four
characteristics.

First, such a moment is a moment of real need, and a
real need means an anxiety without a way of escape. It
is not necessary here to think only of our danger from
death.   We suffer from many patent and latent perplexities. We carry them with us every day; sometimes
we are their cause, sometimes their victims.   We stand
before barred doors and cannot open them.   There are
our failings or secret shackles which we cannot lose.
Such moments of deep and real anxiety can lead us to a
decision before God.

To be sure, it ought not to be necessarily so.   Good
fortune, days of joy and life on the so-called mountain
tops, could serve as occasions for meeting God.   Ordi-
narily our times of ease do not lend themselves for such
decisions.   For while at such times God is indeed with
us, we are not with Him.   We are with ourselves, full
of our own interests and fired by our own will and
strength.   Only out of the depths do we cry unto God;
we seek Him only in our need.   When we are compelled to seek Him we must come down from our
heights.

When we are made to bend low on knees we are
small and humble enough for God.   Yes, when the
need of God comes over us the glory of man fades away.
A final restlessness takes hold of us and a wound burns
secretly within us.   It is then that I become aware that
I, even my piety and goodness, avail me nothing.   Be-

fore Him I am become as dust. Before Him I am nothing. God himself, God alone, must become my all. The
waves roll high in our soul. Our misery becomes well
nigh fathomless, even if good fortune should appear to
smile on us. But here, just here, God can become for
me what He is for me in the day of gladness and in
nights of sadness: my Saviour who has mercy on me.

Second, it is always Jesus Christ in whom all these
things are true. It is always Jesus Christ who turns to
me as my Saviour who has mercy on me. To be sure,
it is none other than God, and God alone, who saves.
But it is God entering into the place of my guilt—God
who has mercy on me; God who does not stay with
Himself but who in compassion steps forth and turns to
me. Here is Jesus Christ. For Jesus Christ is and
means God, but God at the place of my guilt; God with
me in my deep misery; God for me and not for Himself.

What we really know of Him and whatever help we
have from Him in our sorrow, sin and death, we know
and have in Jesus Christ. The disciples were troubled
when they saw Jesus walking on the water. They thought
it was a ghost. But it was neither ghost nor phantom.
And neither is it an illusion that God is with me in my
need. God without Jesus Christ, God only in our
thoughts and feelings or in some home-made portrait
such as "religions" offer, such gods are illusions indeed.

Their God is a ghost, a phantom and a delusion, a far-
away and unapproachable God. But now He is really
with us, as near to us as only the dearest and best of

friends is near us in an hour of direst distress. Do you ask "Who is this friend in need? What is His name? Where will I see Him who is my helper and the captain of my salvation?" Lo, His name is called Jesus Christ; and none other will you see standing before you than Jesus, Jesus the man from Nazareth. As incomprehensibly as He came across the waves to stand before His disciples will He stand before you. And then? Yes, then *we* also will have to let it become true that He who is with us is not a ghost and not an illusion, but the Lord.

Closely related to our second consideration is the third. Since it is God who is really with me in my real need, because He is with me in my guilt and my despair, in my scruples and accusations; because He is with me in the bottomless depths from which I see no escape, He is a God who doeth wondrous things. He is a God who makes a way out of my depths for me. No lock or bolt is so strong that He cannot break it. There is no prison door which He cannot cause to fly open. He breaks the jaws of death and makes hell itself to disgorge its victims. For His sake, anxieties and sorrows, storms and waves, yea, even the night, are rich in blessedness. Here miracles of mercy will be with you. You do not need to create such occasions and situations.

Life provides enough dark and lonely and fearful days without help from us. Anxious hours of self-accusation come of their own accord. But we are told not to fear them when they come over us. For the

Lord will meet us there; He is waiting there for His own. We all desire to meet God; but we would meet Him without these harrowing anxieties; without the horrors of the bottomless pit! We are too much afraid of them. We are too well satisfied in our so-called ease to leave it behind us; we are too complacent on our thrones to come down to our level. And for this very reason we must forego the blessedness of meeting God who is waiting to come near to us.

Jesus Christ is today the same as yesterday; but we are much too safe and secure to be really shaken by Him. Even in our misery we are still too strong in ourselves to cling to Him alone; and in our manly daring we are still so rashly arrogant that we refuse to become so radically daring as to lay hold only on Him.

I might say—and this is our fourth consideration—we are not obedient enough to become really free of our anxieties and pride. Our want of obedience will not permit us to be rid of our human rashness and despair. At first glance Peter seemed foolhardy and presumptuous when he stepped out of his boat on the waves in yonder anxious hour. But he obeyed the word of Jesus. He did what he did in obedience to Him. It is a part of every decisive moment in the presence of God that a man becomes obedient. What does it mean? It does not mean that I resolve to help myself. It does not mean that by faith and prayer I intensify the degree of my divinity in order to experience help from God. It does mean, however, that I do what I must do because I am commanded to do it.

A command is contrary to my nature, and its fulfilment does not come from my own powers. At any rate, so it was with Peter. He did not mean to exhibit his own daring. If it was only that, his conceit was thoroughly and quickly taken out of him. He acted on command; he had to learn obedience. Our own anxieties invite the question, What do you want? Do we ask for gratification of some desire of our own? Shall fulfilment come from within us? If so, we do not stand in the light of Jesus' help. For the help which Jesus brings is from God. His might is holy might, and it becomes active for a man who wills something higher than himself. Where a man really wills to obey God and wills nothing else, there Jesus helps. Where such a will is wanting, chaos reigns. Left to our own counsels, we perish.

Peter had this experience. He stepped on the water on the command of Jesus. When he forgot it, his walking lost its meaning; and he lost heart. In his need it did not profit him that Jesus was standing before him. He was not looking to Jesus anyway, he was looking to himself. He was comparing his own strength with the dangerous waves and—sank. He may even have felt within him a "do or die" spirit. But he dared something that was beyond his strength. Such rash daring and stubborn defiance to "do at any price" do not count before God. A man's faith in his own will to conquer is vain faith.

In this instance it is quite evident that faith in God's might does not mean rash and daring ventures. It does mean obedience, however. In the storms of our times we do not need rash and daring men; we do need obedient men. There are enough idealists, enough brave souls who mean to change the world; but obedient men are rare. And therefore our world is so dark, so very dark: therefore we are so forsaken in the storms that are shaking our age.

But it must not necessarily remain so. The fathomless depth of our day is our disobedience. Over the turbulent sea of our disobedience Jesus Christ must come to save us. Yes, it is His help, His help for us and our times that He shall break the fetters of our disobedience, and make us free and give us courage not for daring dreams and foolhardy ventures, but for obedience. His help will mean nothing less daring, nothing less brave and courageous, nothing less new and free; for it will mean that we dare to become free for what God wills us to do.

In the beginning of our story we are told that Jesus went into a mountain alone to pray. Coming from this hour of prayer He met His disciples. With Jesus prayer means to search out the will of God. Because He was obedient as none other, He is the only one who does what is wholly new and large as He brings us God's help from God. What concern is it of ours? you ask.

We also ought to walk across the waves at His word. He wants us to live, live in our terrible world where we are surrounded by every care and anxiety, but He does not want us to despair. He makes us live as sinners, as mortals well aware that we are but dust and ashes, at every turn a prey of the grim reaper. But He wants us to know in the very midst of our every affliction that we are God's beloved children; God's poor and righteous people, His redeemed.

As long as we understand His will merely as a religious exhortation which we must fulfil in our own strength, we are lost. In the hour of our real need we shall then be swallowed up. In the very moment, however, when we see and hear it as Jesus' command, yea, as the word of our Saviour who is coming across the waves into my pathless wilderness; when we know that it is His will and work that I shall live, and live my life as a child of the eternal Father—I, even I the sinner; I who must die; I who, forsaken and cast adrift, have even lost courage to live—in the very moment of my obedience to His will I can work alertly, stoutly, courageously and vigorously at the task which He has assigned to me. Aye, in my very weakness I may then become a source of strength for my despairing neighbor.

We can only thank God, and thank Him anew every day, that He has mercy on us as He has joined us in Christ Jesus and given us in Him our victory in life and in death. For God's sake, there are no longer fathomless depths and unendurable misery; for help, help from God is come very near to us!

IV.

FACE TO FACE
WITH THE FINAL QUESTION

And it came to pass, as we were going to the place of prayer, that a certain maid having a spirit of divination met us, who brought her masters much gain by soothsaying. The same following after Paul and us cried out, saying, These men are servants of the Most High God, who proclaim unto you the way of salvation. And this she did for many days. But Paul, being sore troubled, turned and said to the spirit, I charge thee in the name of Jesus Christ to come out of her. And it came out that very hour. But when her masters saw that the hope of their gain was gone, they laid hold on Paul and Silas, and dragged them into the marketplace before the rulers, and when they had brought them unto the magistrates, they said, These men, being Jews, do exceedingly trouble our city, and set forth customs which it is not lawful for us to receive, or to observe, being Romans. And the multitude rose up together against them: and the magistrates rent their garments off them, and commanded to beat them with rods. And when they had laid many stripes upon them, they cast them into prison, charging the jailor to keep them safely: who, having received such a charge, cast them into the inner prison, and made their feet fast in the stocks. But about midnight Paul and Silas were praying and singing hymns unto God, and the prisoners were listening to them; and suddenly there was a great earthquake, so that the foundations of the prison house were shaken: and immediately all the doors were opened; and every one's bands were loosed. And the jailor, being roused out of sleep and seeing the prison doors open, drew his sword and was about to kill himself, supposing that the prisoners had escaped. But

Paul cried with a loud voice, saying, Do thyself no harm; for we are all here. And he called for lights and sprang in, and, trembling for fear, fell down before Paul and Silas, and brought them out and said, Sirs, what must I do to be saved? And they said, Believe on the Lord Jesus, and thou shalt be saved, thou and thy house. And they spake the word of the Lord unto him, with all that were in his house. And he took them the same hour of the night, and washed their stripes, and was baptized, he and all his, immediately. And he brought them up into his house, and set food before them, and rejoiced greatly, with all his house, having believed in God.

—*Acts 16:16-34.*

A monumental story!   In every detail it reminds us of the equally remarkable events which the gospels relate as taking place around the Saviour. As there, so we see here a dark night of human misery. All around us it is night.   But, like a flash of lightning, a single man pierces with one thrust at one place the maddening gloom. *"Believe in the Lord Jesus Christ!"* And suddenly darkness is turned into light. As if to intensify the breath-taking event; as if to prevent all misapprehension that some innocent little incident, something less astounding than a momentous and massive miracle, has come to pass, the light pierces the gloomy night at its darkest spot.   Out of a dungeon, scourged and shackled men cry out the name of Jesus Christ as the name of Him who transforms the world's night into God's bright day.

We are observing Epiphany Sunday today. Epiphany means appearance. The church of old has so named this Sunday in commemoration of the appearance of Jesus Christ on earth. We cannot better observe the day than by letting our story tell us of an epiphany of Jesus Christ. For this Sunday means that in the thick gloom of our human misery resounds the name *"Jesus Christ."* As the bright morning star, He marks the end of the night and the promise of a new day.

Night describes the "heathen world." A dark and gloomy world rises before our mind when we think of it. But let us not look at paganism and its representatives with haughty contempt. If we accompany the apostle Paul on his journeys through the ancient world we find ourselves in the midst of a rich culture. Cities like Philippi, Ephesus and Corinth were the homes of a splendid civilization. Great wealth had accumulated in these commercial centers, and education and many arts flourished there. Do not mistake paganism, either ancient or modern, with lack of culture and want of knowledge and savoir vivre. On the contrary, this pagan world is one of humanity's brightest flowers. Paganism may mean a very high degree of culture and civilization.

We may perhaps compare the "heathen world" of Paul's time with the noble figure of a man who has acquired many a treasure. He has mastered the arts and sciences; with his manly strength he has created a proud and noble civilization. But its outward splendor surely does not deceive us. The soul which gave birth to the knowledge and power of this civilization and to its arts and education is sick, sick unto death. Tragedy is written across its noble face. Three melancholy lines bear witness of the sickness unto death from which this heathen world was suffering. Our story points them out in the jailor's attempt at suicide; in the soothsaying girl; and finally in the inexpressibly terrible money power which looms up behind the soothsaying maid.

What else do these things signify if they do not say that this glorious culture is marred by an unspeakable depth of inward and outward poverty and an unutterable helplessness and despair?

Such malignant growths are not peculiar to the ancient world and its culture; every age and civilization suffers from similar ulcers. Let no mendacious history texts, such as our historians write them, deceive us. They make us believe that the past was a bright and beautiful world. They hide from us the deep shadows which marred its beauty.

Some of us yearningly meditate on old Basel as on a lost paradise. We think longingly of the Swiss Confederacy of yesterday, or of the time of the Reformation, or of mediæval Germany or Italy. But life in those yesterdays was not nearly as sweet and pleasant as we read in books. It was no less difficult and gloomy than it is today. The great mass of the people suffered from the callousness, cruelty and oppression of a few. In reality, history does not show a civilization without a dark substratum. In reality, all so-called culture always was a thin veneer covering up the gloomy background of life.

What did the common people benefit by the arts and

culture of the Renaissance when it flourished at the courts of princes and popes? And today? Who really profits by our modern successes? Does not the same deep and wide stream of tears and sorrow, of sin and guilt, of hunger and misery, roll across our modern world? No, indeed, we have no reason to extol our civilization at the expense of the "heathen world."

Our story tells us of an attempt at suicide. It is estimated that in Germany alone between twelve and twenty thousand people are annually driven to take this melancholy way out of life. What a monstrous power is "suicide." What a staggering sum of anxieties, perplexities and utter despair is included in this suicide list! Why? Why must suicide be? Is it not because good will and kindness and counsel and helpfulness are wanting among us notwithstanding our rich culture?

That Roman official wanted to kill himself because he thought his prisoners had escaped. Why is there no other way for him out of his troubles than this desperate one which offers no escape after all? Simply because he knows that he is held responsible for his prisoners. If they escape he cannot hope for mercy! What a culture! What a society! Governed by notions of honor so barbarous, so coldly murderous as to drive an official to a point where nothing but suicide is left for him! Is there much more mercy among us for those who make a false step in life? Why should not a man make a mistake and fall without being forced to despair? Why is there not a spirit of mercy for the erring one? Why do we not rather conceal his errors and misdeeds? Yes, why not? Mercy means goodness; it means sympathetic understanding; it means to help putting things to rights again.

No, society knows little of these things. I shall remember to my dying day the young man whom a large banking house discharged on account of a slight mistake. He found no other way out of his trouble than a revolver. Cruel are the ways of men with men! Cold and killing are the principles which govern our family life, our business life, our political life. And we make merciless use of them. Yes, the world in which we live is hard and cold and dark.

And now the soothsaying maid. Surely, if in the midst of a rich cultural and also religious age soothsaying flourishes, it is a sign that the deepest problems of men have remained unanswered. Men will then try for answers in dreary and questionable ways. Let us not look contemptuously askance at past ages. A widely read book, telling of the wretched life of the inmates in one of the sanatoria at Davos, describes also in minute detail a spiritualist séance.

These unfortunate people, cultured though they are and claiming with many others of the cultured class to be done with God and eternity, take part in these attempts to lift the veil that hides the secrets of another world. Do they not exhibit one of the common tragedies of modern man: their fear of an impending evil fate? Why do black arts flourish today? Why do people take

to astrology, horology and palmistry?   Why do people
go to soothsayers to inquire about their future?   Can
you not see the perplexities which are besetting our age?

Finally, Paul met this whole gloomy world. As he
wrested the unfortunate maid from the spirits which
possessed her he met a third power.   Money interests
rose menacingly behind the girl.   Woe to him who
touches even one interest of high finance!   The modern
woman of the street is no less their victim than this
soothsaying girl.   Slowly but surely the human vam-
pire kills her body and soul.   But what does human life
matter when money is at stake!   Business must flourish
and vampires must have their dividends!   And when
Paul sought to save the girl he found that the state,
instead of protecting the girl, rose to protect those who
were making profit out of her misery.

The apostle is brought before the court. As a dis-
turber of the public peace he is made to suffer for his
attack on the thrice unholy power of money. He is
scourged and cast into prison, even in the stocks. Can
you see the gloomy darkness which lay on that world?
But, pray, why do we understand this story so well?
Why does it not sound strange and unfamiliar to our
ears?   Is it not because we also are living in a night no
less dark and gloomy than this night of nigh two thousand years ago?

Light pierces the night.   *"Believe in the Lord Jesus
Christ, and thou shalt be saved, thou and thy house."*
Who is Jesus Christ?   Is there a simpler and more

exhaustive answer than the one which we receive here? Jesus Christ is He who is able to scatter the darkness of the world. Can we be told more clearly what we may expect from Him than what we are told in our story? Where one or two men will call upon His name, let their dungeon be ever so deep, light will come to them. Let them but cling to His name! Let them only meet their fellowmen in its power! Let them not fear even if their neighbors are their enemies and tormentors! Darkness shall make way for light. *"Believe in the Lord Jesus Christ, and thou shalt be saved, thou and thy house!"* Yes, believe! Plunge into the darkness of your age in the power of His name. Learn to cling to it as a drowning man will cling to a plank! Let no man, let nothing, take it from you. There *is* salvation. It has been given in His name. Let go of His name— and you are lost. This is Jesus Christ.

But, you may ask, How does Jesus Christ reveal the power of His name? Here is your answer: The jailor, so we are told, was struck by the apostle's word at the very moment when he was about to commit suicide. Demanding a light and casting himself at the apostles' feet, the question pours from his lips, "Sirs, what must I do to be saved?" This is what first happens when Jesus Christ enters the gloom of our life. He kindles a question, an all-embracing question: How shall I be saved?

When we really meet Jesus Christ we are thrown into a deep uncertainty. We are driven to the very edge of a deep precipice where we no longer know how to save ourselves.

There is a large variety of anxieties, doubts and confusions among us. Large is also the host of them who live without counsel and comfort in our modern society. Yes, every one of us is faced with questions and problems which demand solution. But how many of us are really face to face with the last and final question, How shall I be saved? Until we are driven to the last ditch, until it really corners us, this question will little concern us. It is the question which seems to lie so very near today when tremors and convulsions are shaking our age. But although it is the one hopeful sign in our present condition that this question is forcing its way to the surface after a supinely lethargic age has kept it submerged, it has not yet leaped on our tongues. To be saved?

Before we shall ask about it we need to gain just one large insight: that we are lost, completely, irrevocably, eternally lost if—yes, if at the last moment salvation does not come to us. To be lost means that all our efforts, even superhuman efforts, to save ourselves will avail us nothing. To be saved means that another hand must reach out for us, snatch us up and put our feet on solid ground. A simple and elementary insight! It came to the pagan jailor in his terrible suicide night. Do *we* know it? Perhaps we do, but we refuse to admit it. Surely, we are aware of many difficulties. Perhaps we even blame ourselves, and if worst comes to worst we throw ourselves away.

I see men living in fears and doubts. I see many people almost collapsing under a sense of inadequacy and inferiority in the face of their troubles. It is a terrible thing to be under clouds of uncertainty; it is terrible to be in desperate straits almost to the point of insanity. In such distressing situations men know what it means to be inferior, oppressed, afflicted. But do they know what it means to be lost?

We may admit that we are unhappy; but do we admit that we are lost? A man can do it only when he knows that he is not only unhappy but that he is disobedient. Because of my disobedience I am condemned. This is what the modern man will neither know nor admit. He does not even suspect that a final verdict has been passed on him, a verdict which reads: You are not only miserable and afflicted; no, you are a sinful and therefore mortal man. You have lost touch with the fountain of your life, God. Here is the source of all your misery; here is the open sore from which oozes out the sorrow of the world. Disobedience! It is no longer merely inadequacy.

Disobedience means that there is one to whom I belong with all that I am and have. And I? I resist Him in what I am and in what I do. I do not render unto Him what I owe Him—my life and my obedience. I am a rebel! I renounced my king. Therefore I am lost. This is what the jailor discovered in that most terrible hour of his life. I belong to the Lord who has made heaven and earth. And I have never, not even one moment of my life, concerned myself about this

Lord of mine. I am lost. What must I do to be saved?

Do you think our time knows something of it? Do you not see the supercilious smile? They even say that it is merciless to mention and to uncover this deepest reason of the misery of our world. And yet, it is mercy, real and true mercy. For here, at the very point where men will admit that they know of their disobedience; where they confess that behind their misery lies not misfortune but condemnation, punishment from God— there, right there the crisis unto new life is come. Here God is waiting for us in incomprehensible mercy, the same God before whom we are guilty and nothing but guilty. At the place where you have no further excuses to offer, where every answer fails you, He intercedes for you. *"Believe in the Lord Jesus Christ and thou shalt be saved!"*

It is true that you are lost, but truer still that thy sins are forgiven thee. True it is that your life is swallowed up in hopeless darkness, but truer still that He has entered into your darkness. You are no longer left alone there, now He is with you and for you. No, you shall not be lost. No, your rebellion against God and his wrath over you is not His final word. For the Lord before whom you are wholly guilty is also the Lord who has mercy on you. And His mercy is the victory that overcometh the world. Believe in the Lord Jesus Christ. This is what dawned on the jailor of the city of Philippi.

"I should like to believe," you will perhaps say. "But

can I?"   What does it mean to believe?   Does not a
steep and insurmountable mountain rise before us when
we are told, Believe!   Let me assure you that the jailor
did most certainly not climb difficult mountain sides in
that hour.   He could not have accomplished strenuous
feats of strength.   Something took place altogether different from what we read in conversion stories where we
are told how men suddenly and in a miraculous manner
became "believing saints."   To be sure, he did something, but something exceedingly simple, something that
seems very small and insignificant, but it was all that he
could do.   He let himself be told something.   He let
himself be told of Jesus Christ.

It is for this purpose that we are also gathered here.
This is what it means to believe.   I am guilty; but now
I am told that Jesus Christ is for me and for the guilt
of all the world.   Receive it!   Lay hold on it!   Cling
to it as a child will hold a coin firmly gripped because
mother said, Do not lose it!   Let it not be taken from
you!   In guilt and grief, in sorrow and affliction, men
are to hear and know and defend to the bitter end:
Jesus Christ, and there is no salvation in any other.

I will add nothing, and I will take nothing away.
Either is dangerous.   I will stay in my place; I will
endure the whole misery of my life, I will live in the
guilt and darkness of the world but I will hold fast that
He is here.   What He has done for me is my freedom
and my salvation.   And all that is required of me is
said in the words, "Wait thou on the Lord!   Commit

thy ways, all thy ways, unto the Lord!" We always think this is too little. It seems so little to be told, "Thy sins are forgiven thee!" We think so because we have not yet seen how large, how dangerous, how immense the guilt we have heaped on ourselves in the sight of God.

We would not hold it lightly that He removes this mountain as He comes and greets us with one unique word—"Forgiveness!" Whoever does not recognize in this word the last and greatest of gifts which God can give men does most assuredly not know what guilt and forgiveness really are.

"What shall I do to be saved?" To be saved! In its most original meaning it does not only mean what we commonly understand by salvation; it signifies unbounded joy, blessedness immeasurable on account of this salvation. When I become really guilty before God, my life rises before me and stands there as one huge accusation. Whither shall I flee? There is no refuge. It is my own life that accuses me and I cannot offer an excuse for it. It rises before *me*. It haunts me, and I cannot evade it; neither can I stand before it as an idle spectator.

If in this misery and torment of my guilt I let myself be told the name "Jesus Christ" an unspeakable joy comes over me. I am unburdened! I am distressed, but He acquits me. I am accused, but my debt is forgiven. This is joy! And therefore our story ends with these words, *"He brought them up into his house, and set food before them, and rejoiced greatly, with all his house, having believed in God."*   A man or two, perhaps a handful of them, who have learned to believe in Jesus Christ as did this jailor—and immediately a warm stream of joy and love and brotherliness begins to flow. It is important for a whole house, yes, for the whole of society, if a man is saved out of the misery of his guilt. Such men will temper the icy blasts which make the world so uninhabitable. They rouse others. Unexpected and peculiar things begin to happen around them, as peculiar as this that suddenly the prisoner becomes the brother of his tormentor and they sit down together at table to break bread with each other. It is a part of forgiveness that it becomes a power of reconciliation among men.

Do we not see that our only need is a handful of men who really believe in Jesus Christ? Fathers, mothers, pastors, members who cling to God, because their misery and guilt make them cry out for the living God! Yea, and also a youth that searcheth for the living God! When these are again given us, in that day streams of righteousness and peace shall roll through our age and world. It is not God's fault that we are wanting them. Part of our faith in the Lord Jesus Christ is our knowledge that God wants to make known to us His name today, that we may experience His power.

V.

I AM THE LORD

Commit thy ways unto Jehovah; trust in Him and He will bring it
to pass.—*Psalms 37:5*.

We will let this text tell us above all that we have a
Lord who desires that we shall entrust our ways to Him.

"Our ways." This means everything that we human
beings, as our own masters, desire, do and achieve; from
the feelings to which we yield ourselves in this or that
situation in life in the secrecy of our hearts to the bent
or character that we finally give to our whole life. In
the end no man or circumstance can determine or dictate our ways to us. Our ways are really *our* ways. Who
is going to hinder us to be and to do in our inmost selves
what we want to be and do? We are little kings. That
is our right and our dignity and our glory. But that
is also the terrible burden of our human existence.

None will relieve us of the responsibility for the ways
which we enter upon and walk. No one guarantees us
where they will finally lead. In the end, no one can
help us, neither father nor mother, neither brother nor
friend, neither husband nor wife. In the end all of us
must choose our ways and walk them ourselves in a

great loneliness. So both are true: we are royally free, and yet totally forsaken.

But written above both these facts there is the greater truth; namely, that we have a Lord; no, not only a Lord, but—mark it well—the Lord, who alone, and as the highest, is that Lord, with no power above or beside Him. It is our glory that we can walk our own ways as masters, but that we *must* walk them, that is our misery. But this glory and this misery have a limit. The Lord sets the limit, He *is* the limit. In the end no one can dictate our ways to us. No one in the end can help us. But with the exception of one, even Him, the Lord. He *wants* to tell us our ways, He *wants* to help us, and He does it too.

Just there in the final analysis, at that remarkable center of our lives, where we sit proudly on a throne, from which no one can thrust us, and pine away in our imprisonment, where no one can visit us—just there He wishes to accost us, there He wants to be heard by us, in His humiliating and consoling: *"I am the Lord."*

God is waiting to tell us this. He is waiting, ever anew, for us to intrust our ways to Him, that we acknowledge Him as the Lord. He wants to rule in the short life that we have to live. Oh, He is doing it now, for we are in His hand, long before we acknowledge Him. But He does not merely want to rule. He wants to lift, to bear us and to redeem. Therefore He stands before our door as the Saviour and knocks, waiting, to tell us, *"I am the Lord"*; waiting for us to acknowledge Him; waiting for us to give Him His place; waiting for us to love Him as He has first loved us.

That is the waiting of the Lord. We forget it, again and again. We run along so foolishly and do not want to hear *"I am the Lord."* He is like a dark shadow over our lives. But there is not a quarter of an hour but that shadow makes itself felt, a shadow of forgetfulness, of great forgetfulness. We forget that our liberty and our loneliness, our strength and our weakness, our joy and our sorrow, our life and death, all have this one limit—*"I am the Lord."* If we would see this boundary line, if we would bow and be still, we would receive a great peace and we would rise up. We would cry to God in the height of our spirit and pride, and in the depth of our loneliness we would sing His praise. Often we have failed to think of it, and we will fail many times more to remember that we are in God's hand.

Then the Lord of Lords waits in vain upon us. Then our ways are, in little and in great matters, as they are bound to be without the light of His countenance. Then we can sin only in our liberty and die in our loneliness. For He wants to be recognized and loved of us, He wants to be besought, that His countenance shall be upon us. Oh, that His hand may so mightily hold, lead and guide us, that in spite of all our shameful forgetfulness we must again and again remember—*"I am the Lord"!*

God does not wait merely upon us to intrust our ways to Him. He has given us His word, to you and me, yesterday and today, through which He tells us what we have forgotten. We have all reasons to feel badly about ourselves, about our foolishness. But His word is nigh us to make us wise. That word is the mercy through which the Lord leads us to Himself, through which He commands, invites, calls and draws us to recognize Him, to love and beseech Him.

Notice—there it is, this grace which comes to us so living, tangible, strong, even today, in the word of the Holy Scriptures: *"Commit thy ways unto the Lord!"* Hear it, today! Do it, today! *Today* is the day of grace.

You have gone your own ways after the desire of your heart, perhaps with defiantly set teeth, filled with the spirit of one saying: "I dare, I must, I will go my own way." There you simply struck the bounds of your own strength, and you found out that: "Even my trees do not grow clear up into the skies; I will not succeed with my ideas or my strength. Men are setting tasks for me which I cannot master. There are circumstances and fateful situations which I cannot see through and against which I run in vain. I am a puzzle to myself and cannot solve it. If I am a king in my own realm, I am nevertheless a small king, a right miserable upstart of a king."

You had to place your life-stakes back a bit and become a little modest. It is not everything even if you hear this Halt! But at least it is something. The word of God is in and under this acknowledgment, that blessed word about the limits: "Commit thy ways unto the Lord." To the Lord, for He can do what you cannot. He gives strength to the weary and enough power to the impotent. Do not look upon this command to halt as an injury, even if it hurts. There you have it. God has only waited upon you, He has not only supported you, but supported you in such a way that you could hear what you must hear: "I am the Lord!"

You certainly could hear it better this way than without his help. You had to be ashamed of the ways you have walked. That is more than when a man merely realizes that he is a weak human being. You said and did things that were not right, in your great strength and liberty. You came away with a guilty conscience and still have it. How did that come? You did not meet an external hindrance, but you met a holy command. You know that you are a transgressor.

You go your own ways, but an order of things which you know well is resisting you and you feel: "Back of this command there is a will that is holy and almighty, from which I cannot escape. This holy and mighty will opposes my will." Your self is now living in this conflict. Blessed are you if you can no longer get out of this conflict. Thus Israel stood before its God when Moses brought it His law—Israel a people of sinners, with this same rupture in its conscience, yet a holy peo-

ple of God. Now the thing was: "Commit thy ways
unto the Lord!" To the *Lord*, the holy and mighty,
whose goodness begins where our goodness ends, who
makes us disgusted with our ways, even our virtuous
ways, when He shows us *His* ways.

That is not all either. But surely God's word comes
to us in this way, too, even in the humiliation that comes
to us, in the accusation that confronts us, in the judgment under which we see ourselves. Do not forget,
and do not seek to escape, this distress. Stay under this
judgment. The Moabites and the Philistines received
no law which adjudged them sinners; they could go
on living in their own ways. But not so with Israel.
So God deals with His own!

He does not merely wait upon them. Nor does He
merely let them find out their own weakness. He un-
covers their iniquity. He confronts them, holy, wrath-
ful, awful. Because He loves them, and in order that
they may in turn love Him and recognize this: *"I
am the Lord!"* But do not let me continue with a description of these possibilities in which the word of God
can come to us, into our lives. An acknowledgment of
our weakness and our iniquity can be the word of God
and healing grace to us only then, when they are an
acknowledgment of Jesus Christ. It takes something
more; yes, something quite different from our humiliation. There is something more, something quite different from that. It has happened and still occurs that
God Himself speaks outright to us, the miserable and

unrighteous people, that He loves us and that He is with us and we belong to Him, and that nothing, nothing can separate us from Him. This word of God is Jesus Christ, acknowledged and believed as the Son of the living God.

Thus God has spoken His word to us; this is His grace, that He has Himself come to us to call us His children. Right there is the boundary line. There is where our boasting and our despair come to an end. Most likely it is only then that we actually come down from the throne of our liberty and emerge from the prison of our loneliness; then we lay down the weapons of our defiance and the complaint of our despair ceases. Then it is we hear, *"Commit thy ways unto the Lord,"* after we have heard: Jesus Christ, Immanuel, God with us!

When we have heard that God Himself intercedes for us, that He loves us in His Beloved One; us, the miserable, the rebellious, the enemy whom He reconciles with Himself. *"I am the Lord!"* To hear means to hear *this*. To hear means to be thankful— not only to be dismayed or humiliated—but thankful! Is it not true that what has brought us together in this hour as a Christian congregation, in spite of all the ungratefulness of which each one of us must confess himself guilty, is this gratitude for that mighty decisive "God with us" in Jesus Christ? Therefore we hear today this word of grace! Oh, might we really hear it, this "Commit thy ways unto the Lord"!

What does it mean to commit your ways unto the Lord? "Trust in Him, He will bring it to pass," we read. To trust in Him, then, is what this word requires of us and upon which God waits. But we cannot, and we must not, cease to go our own ways, to heed the voice of our conscience, our hearts, our understanding, as best we can; to administer our more or less important duties in a large or small circle, to bear our sorrow, to fight the battle of the spirit against the flesh. But to trust in the Lord is something new, the special thing which is added, when we have heard this word.

To commit one's ways to the Lord means to think, beyond all that we undertake or suffer: At the beginning He stands whose servant or maid I am; in the center He stands again, whose is the wisdom and the power through which my labors and suffering can be blest; at the end He stands again, the great and true King, to whose glory all things should redound. That is what it means to trust in Him.

To trust in God is the vision of the human heart, conscience and understanding, the vision of Him who alone is good, of His will, His coming, His kingdom. There is where man becomes a steward instead of a king, and where he knows that this small station as a steward is better than yonder great one of a petty king. Man has changed from a hermit in prison to a sentinel on the battlement. There is where all within the man becomes a waiting upon the Lord (who has waited so long in vain upon us, and must still wait!). There all becomes expectation, now of His clarity upon our ways; now of His commands to tread the ways; now of His assistance which is needed; now of the success which He will grant; now of the commendation—which He Himself will be. And let me say that for the one who trusts in Him that great loneliness, which had been both proud and sorrowful, will be over.

He opens his eyes and is no longer alone, but in the fellowship of the saints who, like him, have come out of great error and tribulation, and, like him, have no other hope but this hope. Herein will lie the proof that we are no longer alone in relation to God; namely, in that we know we are no longer alone among men either, but that we are, together with many others, safely and securely placed in the service of God's holy church.

We must not forget, however, that there is a judgment involved in this trusting in God, a judgment from which one would often like to run away as far as his feet will carry him. To walk my own way day after day with firm step, thinking, speaking, working as long as it is day, as indeed I should, and yet, with it all, to expect nothing of myself, but to await all things from Him Who stands at the beginning, the center and the end; to lay all into His hand and then only to pray that everything may *stay* in His hand; to be moved by His hand alone, so that I will not fall back and do not become my own master again—that means: to die! To have to live and to realize so fully that it is all over with ourselves, as that we can only implore and pray, that means: to die.

No one is more homeless, more uprooted, no one must so live from hand to mouth as that man on whom the miracle of God's word has been performed; that man who, like the widow of Sarepta, has committed his ways unto the Lord and trusts in Him. Concerning this judgment, the close of our text speaks a mighty word: *"He will make it well."* In the original it is much plainer: *"He will do it."* He, not *we*. Much less could we do it "well," in purpose, in means, or in results. We would not do it well. We would, in all probability, not do it at all. In all our doing and suffering we would reach an impasse in the sin and need of our human life. He will do it. He will do it well. What a dethroning of man! He who commits his ways unto the Lord and trusts Him bows under this judgment. We would not have heard the word of God in Jesus Christ if we refuse thus to bow ourselves.

This humiliation experienced by those who have heard God's word is, nevertheless, an exaltation. He will, "He will bring it to pass." This means that the eternal, strong, holy, living God intercedes for them, for the weak ones, for the sinners, for the ungrateful. They do not look into empty space when they look beyond themselves. They look upon Him who has given Himself to them.

He gives them the command which they no longer

can and will give to themselves and He makes them wise in their foolishness. He bears what they cannot bear, and when they break down He does not let them despair. His is the kingdom and the power which they serve even when their work goes to ruin under their very hands, as happens, in the end, even to the best of us. He will, He will bring it to pass! Here the hope of grace reaches down into the midst of judgment. Here is joy in Him in the midst of affliction, and peace in the midst of unrest.

Dear friends, think upon this: Samuel slept as the word of the Lord came to him. He slept as well or as poorly as old Eli slept, to whom the word of God did not come. It was sheer grace that it came to Samuel. And it is grace, when it comes to us. Let us, if it comes to us, answer—the only possible answer, because it expresses a readiness—*"Speak, Lord, thy servant heareth!"*

VI.

THE MYSTERY OF THE GOSPEL.

With all prayer and supplication praying at all seasons in the Spirit, and watching thereunto in all perseverance and supplication for all the saints, and on my behalf, that utterance may be given unto me in opening my mouth, to make known with boldness the mystery of the gospel, for which I am an ambassador in chains; that in it I may speak boldly, as I ought to speak.—*Ephesians 6:18-20.*

Paul sets before us a few great problems of life—namely, the problem of the relation between husband and wife, between children and parents, between master and servant, or, as we say today, the problem between employer and employee. Paul wrote very seriously about these things. Man's grave plight is brought out, hard pressed as he is by the dark powers which overshadow and wreck his life. But, remarkable as it is, always a note of hope did ring through it all again and again which does not escape the ear. Paul speaks seriously, but nevertheless with confidence. "Yes," he says, "an evil day has come upon us, but you shall stand in that evil day. Yes, these are difficult times, but that cannot fell you to the ground. Yes, a mysteriously strong enemy has arisen against us, but you have been

given an armor in the strength of which you can with-
stand this enemy."

Why does Paul speak so hopefully? Not at all
gloomily, and like one who is helpless! Simply because—and this is the mystery of his message—because
he is permeated with the nearness, the mighty presence,
of God, of the living God, with us humans. God has
laid His hand upon men again. This is the "Gospel";
this is Jesus Christ. Because that is true, and just because of it, we are in these hard battles of light against
darkness into which we have been pulled. Times are
so difficult because God's truth is beating a path again
on this earth. But, therefore, this is also a great time.
"Years of decision" are upon us, not because economics
and politics have entered a crisis. Just the reverse—
it is because God has stepped upon the scene again that
the demons are beginning to come to life. For that
reason things are not at all hopeless, but, rather,
hopeful.

There is something deeply fundamental about hope
and the act of hoping in the Bible. Nowhere do we
find so absolutely serious and critical a view of the
plight of man as in the Bible. Nowhere does the grave
accusation that can be brought against us human beings
rise so threateningly as in the Bible. Nowhere is the
superficial philosophy of life so completely surrendered
as in the Bible. Nowhere are we seen so realistically,
so small, so impotent, and so exposed. Nowhere is the
power of the forces that have dominion over us rated as

so awful as in the Bible, be these forces war, mammon, unemployment, sickness, passion, "nerves," or faults. And yet, and in spite of it all, nowhere is the whole restless confusion of human life placed so unreservedly, so fundamentally, so boldly, and so authoritatively into the light of a great hope as in the Bible.

The Bible thinks essentially hopefully about man. All because the Bible thinks fundamentally about *God*. God in the beginning, God in the end, and God in the center.   God lives, and God lives!   Thus we could sum it all up.   And in the Bible it says continually, "He lives, not for Himself, but lives for us."   He emerges from His self-centeredness and turns toward us humans.   Upon this turning of God from Himself to us, upon this the Bible centers itself.   That is its whole message.   For that reason the Bible is fundamentally hopeful.   God lives—and I am in His hands! Or, as someone who thought very deeply about this hope of the Bible concerning man has already expressed it: Man is God's!   That is the way God thinks.

A person might *not* think so fundamentally about God, too.   But that would mean nothing less than to think hopelessly all the time.   Then one simply proceeds with his thinking from man.   Then one sees man at the beginning and man at the end.   Let us say we are looking at the good, the true, the life which man has about him, and then be heartened to try to awaken and develop this good, this true and this life which he has in him.   But what of God?   Oh, then God is He who complements what man lacks with His divine power, goodness and truth, and adds to man, so that man may be better and have more life. But that is everything but thinking fundamentally of God.

The Bible says, "All this good and this life need not be disputed away from us, but it does not save us." With all of it we remain, with our own righteousness, still a thousand miles below that which God wants us to be. But what helps us is that God—even God, I could almost say—comes down over this distance of a thousand miles to us. He does not drop us. This righteousness *of God*, which is awarded us, is what saves us. To think fundamentally about God means to think about Him in such a way that all this good, this true and this life about man does not come into consideration; it is as nothing compared to the fact that God has laid His hand upon him. Man lives by this, and by this alone.

We might think about the sin, the foolishness, the error of man in the same way and yet not think fundamentally about God. Then we see only the evil, see that which is wrong, the passions, the stains and faults of man. But we see them with a false seriousness, with a clouded seriousness, because we do not see what God has done and still does anew for him. Then we abandon man. Maybe we feel that a *few* will be saved from the deluge of corruption. But the masses will go down in their godlessness. The Bible says, "your godlessness, your sins, passions, all of these dark prisons in which you lie—even all this does not ruin you. For God can prove Himself mightier than all that." But, in that you will not see what God is doing for you, *that* could ruin you forever.

We could perish for that we do not see God's hand that is laid on us, *that* holds us *even* in the dark torrent of our sins. Our righteousness will not save us. *God* saves us! Our sin does not destroy us, but our disbelief in God—that could become our ruination. Thus the Bible thinks about God basically; and it therefore thinks hopefully of man.

It makes an enormous difference whether we approach man from the angle of what God does for us or not. If we do not do that we will see—men groaning under a thousand burdens and needs. In the end we too can do nothing else than groan with them. Occasionally we can work up a little joy, perhaps, but in reality all remains dark. But if we should think essentially from God's angle, then all becomes bright. God's light then falls upon men beforehand, whoever they may be. Even then we can still be aware of the difficulty; if anything, we will really see by the brightness of this light more than ever into and down into the depths of sin and error.

Looking out from this great "beforehand," we can no longer overlook the fact that the world in all those errors, and all this imprisonment, is secretly living on the freedom and truth that have come from God into our midst. Then we can no longer overlook the fact

that men are living, even in the darkest places where
they must live, on God's light, which is so strong that
there is no depth into which it would not penetrate.
Even the seriously sick, the hopeless, the demented in
insane asylums, also the suicides in their despair, they
all live, without knowing it, on this one thing: Man
is God's.

In our text Paul calls this truth by the simple name
of "gospel," glad tidings. And glad tidings they are.
That is a truth that must be delivered, cried out in all
the streets. A truth that must break forth and penetrate into all prisons and depths wherever men live.
A truth which simply does not bear lying around in
corners, unpublished, dust-covered, forgotten. It is
this that the apostle is eager about—namely, that this
truth be really delivered, that it become a message to
men. It is as if toward the close of his epistle he saw
before himself man's entire plight in an incomparably
simple way.

There is the world, a dark chamber, a horrible place
with awful prisons and with ways of life that are nothing but enigmas. And now, Paul thinks, the world
waits. It is waiting as though for nothing else, for this
healing, liberating message of truth to come to her.
The world is full of questions—economic, educational,
political, man and woman questions; they all converge
in this one inquiry after this truth of God, which alone
can answer it. And now there is just one thing lacking,
thinks Paul—namely, men who will hear this truth

and pass it on, who will receive it and utter it, have it in them and let it flow forth. There is a lack of people ready to live for this truth, to force a passage for it. Into this work he calls his church, and calls us.

Paul also calls this truth, the truth of the gospel, a "secret." A secret is something that lies hidden, covered up, and which therefore must be hauled forth and, so to speak, brought out of a deep shaft to the light. Thus it is with this truth, that God's hand rests upon humanity. It, too, lies hidden, covered up. It must be brought to the light of day. It is not a simple truth easily found. We do not read it in the papers. We do not find it in books. For this truth is not present in the mind, in the thoughts, of men, or in their conceptions of truth. It is rather another truth that dominates, a truth which is no truth: this truth that is a lie, that there is no God, and therefore no hope for man. Now God's truth must break into the mind of man as into a stronghold that is to be taken by force of arms. Then a struggle arises in the mind of man.

The old lie offers defensive resistance to the new spirit of truth. This struggle, that is, the scene that takes place as often as God's truth comes to us and drives away the false, mendacious thoughts about the world and life which we think—this struggle takes place as often as we meet in church to open ourselves to the message of the Gospel. To listen to a real sermon, therefore, is no small matter. Then God's spirit of truth wants admission. Then we must give up and

lay down whatever within us offers resistance to the
spirit.   The despotic rule of our former thoughts is
being overthrown, the new truth set up in its place.   To
listen to a sermon, therefore, is not merely a matter
of being enlightened a little about God and man but
to be pulled into the conflict where steel clashes with
steel.   God's truth wishes to be victorious, and the
spirit of the times and the spirit of the world must
out!   In every sermon that is a real sermon there is
some casting out of demons!

Furthermore, we must say that preaching the gospel,
the coming to the fore of God's truth, is always an
occurrence, an event.   The truth of God, no doubt,
is true, too, irrespective of us; it wants to become true
among us, by gaining entrance here and there with
some person who surrenders to truth.   In order that
this may come about we must go to a particular place.
As the fiery heat in the earth's interior breaks forth here
and there, as a mountain smokes and a crater forms
where we can come upon this heat, thus also the glow-
ing fire of God's truth has broken forth at some place.
This place, this breaking forth on the part of God's
truth in this world, that is the place of the Saviour,
that is Jesus Christ Himself.

Since He has been here, this truth dwells among us.
Since then death has lost its power.   Since then the
demons are expelled and man freed, because he is
acquitted.   But this event of Jesus Christ is not a
settled thing; it wants continually to occur anew.

Jesus Christ wishes always to break anew into this world, wishes always to make known His truth to ever new persons. Because it is thus, the gospel remains an event. We cannot say "I *have* the gospel now *once for all time;* now I am done, now I have it in my possession." On the contrary, in the face of it we can behave only as we would in relation to an event; questioning, knocking at the door and striving and hoping to have it unfold itself anew for us, again and again, in that it comes to pass anew again and again.

The apostle Paul himself did not have the gospel in his hands once for all. Also in him a battle had to be decided anew in favor of God's truth. Therefore he says of himself expressly, that it must be "given" unto him to preach the gospel. He also had to be prepared anew for Him who wishes to come to him with His truth, even Jesus the Lord. Here it must be admitted that this quality of the gospel of being a secret and an event unfortunately has long been forgotten in our church, and perhaps that is the deepest secret of our weakness.

Again and again we have made of God's truth a ready-made, settled thing of which we fancy ourselves the masters, which theologians have in charge and which preachers offer for sale. That is what has made this truth so impotent and lifeless. There the spirit and the power left the word and it became empty, cold and dead. We can then still speak and hear, but the right kind of hearing and speaking—namely, that

speaking which is battling, that victorious hearing, no
longer take place. We have all suffered under that
condition, have we not? Because this real speaking and
hearing have become so rare in our church. Again and
again there are prolonged periods in the history of the
church when the word of God is dead.

The Bible is there; there is praying, but no power
goes forth from this praying, no salvation from this
truth. And then again it happens that the door opens
suddenly and Jesus Christ speaks His word Himself,
so that men are moved by it and there is a flash of light
as of that one first victory of God's word that took
place in those days when Jesus walked on earth.

So now we understand that the apostle is troubled
about his apostleship. He earnestly desires that all
might be well with his preaching of the gospel; that
when he opens his mouth God's word may break forth
"joyfully." Just so we need not talk into empty
space! Rather not speak at all! Just so we do not have
to listen and yet not hear! Rather hear nothing at all
than empty, dead sermons, which result in turning
away from God rather than in turning to Him. Rather
nothing at all than that, rather less talking and hearing, and in its place a kind of speaking of God and
hearing of His truth that flow out of this listening to
the secret of this truth. That is Paul's standpoint when
he says to his congregation: "Pray ye at all seasons."
He summons us to cooperate with him.

It is not true that the apostle, or, as his successor,

the minister, alone is responsible that the word of God be alive among us. That is the condition in the church, is it not—that we have the ministers that we deserve? If we approach the hearing of God's word as mere onlookers, not in earnest, not participating, then we will not hear anything and nothing will transpire. Thus we all have a joint responsibility; thus we, the church, are the workshop where the real hearing and movements of the living word of God are to go on. "Pray ye!" says Paul. To pray means nothing other than to react in downright earnest, personally, unreservedly to this truth: God lives and I am in His hands.

The point is to carry about with us this truth not as dead truth but as truth that is becoming, ever growing, truth for us. This can come about in no way other than that you go to this God and talk to Him, knowing that He hears you. Talk to Him as the child to the father. There where there is prayer there is also entering into the "becoming-reality" on the part of truth. To pray means to know: "God is lacking (in my life); His truth must come entirely new; to that end I would like to give myself, be a door, perhaps a tiny, tiny door, or, if God will give it, a big open door, through which the truth of God may enter, living, into the life of many men." Therefore pray ye!

That is what is meant by this word "Watch ye," too! To watch means to be mindful of life, of the people, the things, the times; to regard it all attentively, so that one can get to the bottom of things and perceive the great lack of God. Then go to praying again, to supplicate for God's spirit and God's truth. Such people God needs, says Paul. Such people are openings through which God's truth can break a path in this world.

Thus it stands facing us, the task of the church in our time, too. Also today; yes, today, the world is waiting for the gospel. People are inquiring, searching all the time; there is a restless looking about in anticipation that has found many expressions, and to which only God's truth can give, and can be, the answer. Who shall give the world that answer, if not the church of Jesus Christ, which is in its midst? The world will go to rack and ruin if the salt of this answer is withheld. What did they say about John Wesley, who in his day shook whole cities with his message, but that he saved England a revolution? That is saying a good deal, perhaps too much. One thing, however, is plain: We too are, in the midst of the awful revolutions of our period, as those who owe the word of God to the people of our day. If we, the church, shirk our obligation, then we too will perish in the deluge of wrong and violence which will irrevocably break forth where God's word and truth die out.

Why are we so inert? Why do we watch and pray so little in order that to our preachers and also to ourselves the Word might be given, that "utterance might be given unto me in opening my mouth—with boldness"?

Basically the Bible thinks hopefully of man, because it thinks from God's angle. We should feel ourselves much more called unto this hopeful thinking from God's angle. That is apostle's work, that is Saviour's work. For such work the church should be the right place. Could it not be that decisive help, reaching clear into the things economic and political, proceeded even today from no other place than this one, called the church, from a church that once more knows about the secret of her gospel?

VII.

MISERABLE LAZARUS

Now there was a certain rich man, and he was clothed in purple and fine linen, faring sumptuously every day: and a certain beggar named Lazarus was laid at his gate, full of sores, and desiring to be fed with the crumbs that fell from the rich man's table; yea, even the dogs came and licked his sores. And it came to pass, that the beggar died, and that he was carried away by the angels into Abraham's bosom: and the rich man also died, and was buried. And in Hades he lifted up his eyes, being in torments, and seeth Abraham afar off, and Lazarus in his bosom. And he cried and said, Father Abraham, have mercy on me, and send Lazarus, that he may dip the tip of his finger in water, and cool my tongue; for I am in anguish in this flame. But Abraham said, Son, remember that thou in thy lifetime receivedst thy good things, and Lazarus in like manner evil things: but now here he is comforted, and thou art in anguish. And besides all this, between us and you there is a great gulf fixed, that they that would pass from hence to you may not be able, and that none may cross over from thence to us. And he said, I pray thee therefore, father, that thou wouldst send him to my father's house; for I have five brethren; that he may testify unto them, lest they also come into this place of torment. But Abraham saith, They have Moses and the prophets; let them hear them. And he said, Nay, father Abraham, but if one go to them from the dead, they will repent. And he said unto him, If they hear not Moses and the prophets, neither will they be persuaded, if one rise from the dead.—*Luke 16:19-31.*

Dear hearers: Let me say in advance that I will

be able to give an exposition of only a part of the previously read text. It contains too much, so that in the period of one sermon there is room for only a little of what might be said. I have read an entire series of Luther's sermons on this parable and did not get the impression that even he had mastered the subject in one sermon hour. So I feel pardonable for taking only a section and, if very imperfectly, speaking about the miserable Lazarus and his remarkable position in this gospel. It does not appear that he is the chief personage in this story, and yet it is so. One must first understand him, and from that understanding go on to understanding the peculiar sin and punishment of the rich man. But these shall remain in the background for us today.

Let us begin with the last words of our text, which tell us that the brothers of the rich man who are still living ought to hear Moses and the prophets. *What* should they learn of Moses and the prophets, as long as there is time, and *what* should *we* learn of Moses and the prophets? We read what should be the indubitable answer to this question in the first part of Luke's gospel, in the magnificat of Mary: "His mercy is unto generations and generations of them that fear Him. He hath showed strength with His arm; He hath scattered the proud in the imagination of their heart. He hath put down princes from their thrones, and hath exalted them of low degree. The hungry He hath filled with good things; and the rich He hath sent empty away. He hath given help to Israel, his servant."

That is what we learn of Moses and the prophets, while there still is time. But what does that mean? It does not merely mean that God has taken up our cause, has revealed Himself to us, has come to us and abides with us with the immeasurable beneficence of His presence and sovereignty, but it means that this is the designated way and the designated manner according to which He does all things. "He hath descended into the lower parts of the earth." He abides "with those of broken and humble spirit." He makes the dead to live, and calls that which is not into being. Is it not so? It is of this condescension of God toward a people that was no people, that Moses, the man of God, bore witness; it is about this choice of the miserable that the prophets witnessed.

Who is this servant of the Lord, about whom they preached: "He hath no form nor comeliness; we looked upon him, but there was no beauty that we should desire him?" And when the time and the prophecy were fulfilled, there was the fulness of all God's word and God's presence: the child in the stable in Bethlehem, the Son of Man, who had no place where He could lay His head, who was ostracized in the name of God and crucified in the name of Cæsar. "In our needy flesh and blood the eternal God was mantled." Immanuel—"God with us"—in the Holy Scriptures from begining to end means: Lazarus, the miserable, who lay before the door of the rich man, full of sores. Who seeks Him, called God, in the Holy Scriptures, must seek Him in Lazarus.

Because the rich man left Lazarus lying at the door, and did not, or would not, see him, therefore he did not find God; and for that particular reason he found himself in hell and torment. Do not let Lazarus lie at the door, do not overlook him and do not pass him by. For time and eternity hinge upon this fact for you. Therefore, do not do it! See, there, and nowhere else, is the tabernacle of the Lord with men! That is what we should learn of Moses and the prophets, as long as there still is time.

Who is Lazarus? The name signifies "one who needs the help of God." This Lazarus lay at the door of the rich man, full of sores, and desired to satisfy his hunger with the crumbs that fell from the master's table. And now let us come to the heart of the matter. Lazarus is for you the man who is dependent upon you, or the one you meet who in any way needs the help of God, where God has already helped you. Always, it is the fellowman who lacks what you have; always, the fellowman who desires to be satisfied with what falls from your table, over against whom you stand as a rich man.

Perhaps it is just so, or nearly so, as described in the parable—for the story is a parable—that we are rich and well-to-do. Do not say immediately that you are out of the question then. Do not try to shield yourself with the fact that you are not clothed in purple and costly linen, and do not fare sumptuously every day; that you do not belong to the well-to-do, let alone that you are wealthy. There are really few poor people among whom there are not others who are still poorer than these, and in whose sight the poor are rich. Most of us might, in this respect, customarily be classed with the middle, or citizens', class of more modest means. Even this citizenry is talking today of hard and threatening times, and not unjustly so.

Let us not deceive ourselves. Lazarus lies at our door, and from his viewpoint our conditon is certainly not hard and precarious; this Lazarus, who would very gladly exchange with our civilian's cares—an exchange which we would not seriously care to make; Lazarus, who looks on while we treat ourselves, or think we safely may treat ourselves, to things that are in his eyes much less indispensable than in ours, the while Lazarus simply does not get the things which are really much more nearly indispensable; Lazarus, the restless, the dissatisfied proletarian of our streets over there, the jobless who in spite of his unemployment insurance is not so well off as it might appear to this or that onlooker; Lazarus, who shamefacedly begs everywhere, slinking from door to door; and Lazarus who is too proud for that, too—and then for us to come with accusations!

God knows what might be justly said against Lazarus. And if there is ten times as much to be said against him—this one thing the Rhine would not wash away, namely: He is there, he lies at our door. We have, and he has not. He is miserable, while God has helped us. Now, do not ask: "Yes, but what shall we *do* for him?" This is the question wherewith we so often defend ourselves, when we are determined to do nothing!

We are not concerned here primarily with *doing;* primarily we are concerned with seeing, with knowing, with hearing the call to rise, with being awake. Don't you see that you are better off than thousands and thousands of others, and do you not know that for that reason everyone of these thousands and thousands, in so far as he meets you and stands before you in your path, is the man in whom no one less or other than God may be found of you, God with all His gifts—or you will never find Him? Do you see that? All action of which we are not now talking may flow out of this "seeing."

But this parable does not speak merely of money and goods. This wealth is certainly not the highest, and this sort of need of Lazarus is certainly not the greatest or the worst. See, you may be rich in love, friendship and honor which have come a-flying to you on all sides. Perhaps you have somehow in you and about you, without any effort on your part, a something which makes folks like to have you around, or like to be around you, in so much that you never feel lonesome or foresaken, because you are surrounded and carried along by people in whom you trust, and on whom you can count.

Happy are you! You rich man! How many of those who possess villas and autos must envy you! Because they and many others lack what you are rich in. Yes, this Lazarus is to be found in all walks of life: Lazarus the unlovable, the unloved; Lazarus the awkward and the bore, who unfortunately is driven to revolve around himself and who allows the best opportunities to trickle through his fingers, whom no one can help, because he cannot under the most favorable conditions help himself; Lazarus, who for this and many other reasons has nobody to help him. And you, you have someone, perhays many—you are better off just by yourself and still better off with others.

You are the rich man and he lies before your door with sores. God has helped you, just along the very lines in which this man is so needy. Do not calm yourself by seeking to escape by means of an argument that in many other ways he is not so badly off, perhaps better off than you are. In this one respect—and there is no gainsaying it—you are better off. And now, just make this entirely clear to yourself: You will either find God and His gift in and together with this Lazarus or you won't find them at all—with all your enchanting lovableness, amid the general esteem and friendship that surround you.

This wealth could lie deeper too. Perhaps you are not only lovable and popular but a thinking, serious, genuine man. You have principles. And not only that, but you understand how to tread your path of life in all straightforwardness and wholesomeness. You know how to discriminate. You keep your hands off the crude or fine plays of the theatre. You know your limitations and go about quietly to prove yourself a master in self-restraint, after Goethe's idea. Lucky man! Rich, very rich man! More people envy you than you think, would like to nourish themselves with the crumbs that fall from your table. They would like to have what you possess securely but mysteriously. And they have it not.

They lie before your door as miserable Lazaruses: there is the foolish Lazarus, who does not know what to do with his life and powers; the shallow and flippant Lazarus, who never achieves anything and throws what is given him out of the window; the thoughtless, rash Lazarus, who does not understand himself and therefore not the world and always plays the wrong card; Lazarus, the man who lives on mere make-believe, and because he does is dead certain to live himself into some disappointment of a lighter or graver nature, if it has not already come upon him with all the severity by which life usually avenges itself upon those who do not wish to take life seriously.

You rich man in your complete genuineness, you know that there is such a Lazarus with wounds, don't you? You cannot be content to think that he is disgusting to you, can you? That you would rather pass

him by with a pitying shrug of the shoulders?   He is
disgusting to you, and rightly so!   To pass this Lazarus
by is the most likely thing one would do.   But don't
you at the same time know and think about these words:
"Descended into the lower parts of the earth?"   Descended to those who needed His help—not to the
healthy who need no physician!   That very thing the
partisan and patron of Lazarus is the eternal, living
God Himself.

Should you, even in the deepest seriousness, pass him
by, you have passed God by; if you will have nothing
to do with him, then you do not care about God and
will not find Him in all eternity.   Here, and here
only, is where God waits for you.

Let us suggest a fourth consideration.   According to
the Holy Scriptures there is a richness in God.   Nothing
superficial should be understood here.   Not that which
one calls piety—today a rather contemptuous term—
neither is it mere emotionalism and certainly not mere
morals and intellectual belief.   No, your wealth can
be the true wealth—true, living, sane, the wealth of
Christian faith, which is created through and sustained
by the Holy Spirit, which makes one righteous and
blessed before God, because in this faith we have all
that we need be before God.

How insignificant is all other wealth, compared with
that of the man who dares to say these two little words:
"I believe—because I know in whom I believe!"   Now
perhaps there lies at the door of such a rich man a

Lazarus who is rich in everything else but who is poor, especially in God; Lazarus who does not believe, who perhaps says "I cannot believe!" perhaps publicly says "I will not believe!" It may be that even now we ourselves are lying outside with such an "I-can-not!" or "I-will-not!" person.

We would undoubtedly not be here if we had not already been inside through true faith, rich in God, and if we did not at least hope once again to be on the inside. But if we just for one moment think of ourselves as being on the inside, then there are over against us others who are on the outside, with annoying doubt, or with most annoying opposition, or, worse yet, who go their way in absolute indifference, apparently sufficient unto themselves with their business, their petty or important duties, problems and joys of their existence; who do not care about God, at least not seriously, and frankly dispense not only with the highest and the best but with the "one thing needful"; who with closed eyes walk to eternal ruin.

Is such a one also a Lazarus in the sense of the Gospel? Does the same law hold good here? Even when such a Lazarus does not conduct himself peacefully in his need, but begins to beat against the door of the rich man; even if it comes to exalting unbelief over belief in God, as it is now being done in Soviet Russia on such a grand scale and which they frankly desire to transplant into Germany. One does not gather that Catholic and Protestant Christianity have yet seen a Lazarus in this needy man. If we did we would not speak of a "religious front" or of "counter-thrusts" which are now to be undertaken against the propaganda of unbelief. What would be the sense of creating a "front" against him?

The rich man must certainly do something else toward this boisterous brother on the outside, if he realizes that it is his brother, the miserable Lazarus, who conducts himself so outspokenly ugly toward our Most Holy One. But, then, who is not the miserable Lazarus? Over against whom are we better off than just this cultured, or crude, this quiet or boisterous "godless" one? In what are we rich, if not exactly in this case? Where have we been helped so visibly and mightily, where on the other hand is this need so great? And if that is true of the needy one, and if on the other hand the truth is valid—"descended into the lower parts of the earth"; if God is all along the line precisely and without any question the God of the needy, and if Christ still is being mantled in our needy flesh and blood—can we imagine ourselves to be rich in God without realizing that we cannot by any means get rid of the atheists, nor consider it our first duty to *fight* against them, but rather to take their need upon ourselves, and to seek to see and understand them in all their terrible need?

How terrible it would be if we would live, as Christians, sumptuously every day, clothed in purple and costly linen of faith, were perhaps disgusted but not really disturbed, not concerned about, and not feeling called upon to assume, any responsibility for that misery of godlessness before our doors! How awful, if the very thing that is holiest to us would turn against us and our faith be disclosed as unbelief before the judgment seat of the God of the poor!

But we might ask, "Why is God, the God of the Holy Scriptures, so outspokenly and partially the God of the needy? What does He see in Lazarus, that He is particularly his partisan, that everything about the rich man is determined by the attitude he takes toward Lazarus who needs the help of God?" Let us be careful not to smuggle into the character of Lazarus some hidden virtue. He is absolutely a needy one, a poorest Lazarus. His plight may strike our ears as embarrassing, but the fact cannot be altered that Luther included in the diseases of Lazarus—syphilis!* Whoever wants to make him out bad—his Lazarus—let him make him as bad as he likes. He will have cause enough. But let him also realize, it is *not* a question of the goodness or badness of Lazarus that we are dealing with.

The point in our text is this: God is love, as we have heard in today's epistle. And that love, which is God, is, in contrast to all human love, that kind of love which seeks a person because he is needy and because it can and will help; not because that love needs anyone, not because it has any purpose or design with that or this person—it is an overflowing love that does not

* Weimar ed. 10, III, page 6.

make a person blessed to make itself blessed but is blessed in itself and in that it makes others blessed.

That is why He who is called God in the Holy Scriptures chooses the foolish things and the weak things in the eyes of the world. That is why Christ was born in a stable and died on the cross-beam. That is why Lazarus and not the rich man is the friend of God. That is why the needle's eye is set up for the camels of all the human kingdoms of body, soul and spirit. That is why the rich man cannot be saved, except together with Lazarus, as the brother of the miserable Lazarus. We have not for that reason fully understood the unsearchable ways and the incomprehensible judgments of God. We have only said: "These are God's judgments, and these are God's ways and they are answer to every Why?"

And now we follow up with two words in relation to the human side of the secret of Lazarus. First, this is certain: the whole situation in which Lazarus found himself, as one who merely needs, and is anticipating God's help (*i.e.*, not entitled to it)—as far as there is help of God for him—this whole situation bespeaks better the position of men with relation to God, instead of the situation of the rich man over against God, whatever we may think his wealth to be, provided that man, who has made himself guilty of death, stands before God as a traitor. We have not spoken of that particularly today. But the Bible tells us that, directly or indirectly, on every page.

If that holds good, what does that imply as to the wealth of all rich men? Is Lazarus not in a much more true and genuine sense a true human being than the rich man? Is it not more comprehensible that God would rather come to dwell with him than with the rich man, though there be no merit attached because of his poverty? Is it not high time that the rich man recognize in Lazarus the pattern of Christ, without which there can be no salvation for him in spite of wealth? And then Lazarus, in contrast to the rich man, has not the virtue, but the advantage, that in his relationship to his fellowmen he is absolutely dependent for life upon them.

The rich man may forget and ignore him. Lazarus will certainly not forget the rich man, especially when he knows that he is inside seated at the table, and Lazarus will not ignore him, when he passes him by in his contentment and security. That the dogs have mercy on him and lick his sores simply throws light on how much he waits on that human being, that fellowbeing of his within at the table. Certainly he does not wait on him in a neighborly love, but in highest self-love, but nevertheless in all self-love does he actually wait for him.

There also he has an advantage over the rich man. It is not a virtue which he exercises but an advantage of his position as a needy person. But it is an advantage. That is exactly what the rich man does not do. He waits expectantly upon no one; he needs no one, not even his dogs. That is the fateful thing about material, intellectual and spiritual wealth: As rich men we do not need our fellowmen. That is why we do not see Lazarus, nor Christ. He came to seek and to save that which was lost.

Should this not be the natural, so to speak, the well-pleasing attitude on the part of sinful men toward God: that we are dependent upon one another and wait expectantly upon one another? Is not that, and only that, the reason why God descended into lowliness to become a partisan of Lazarus and not of the rich man? Should it not therefore be necessary for us to become brothers of Lazarus? As brothers of Lazarus we would see that we need one another, one Lazarus needing the other, and each and all alike needing Christ. Oh, that we might be made to see!

VIII.

PARADISE LOST

And the Lord God planted a garden eastward in Eden; and there he put the man whom he had formed. And out of the ground made the Lord God to grow every tree that is pleasant to the sight, and good for food: the tree of life also in the midst of the garden, and the tree of knowledge of good and evil. And a river went out of Eden to water the garden; and from thence it was parted, and became into four heads. The name of the first is Pison: that is it which compasseth the whole land of Havilah, where there is gold; and the gold of that land is good: there is bdellium and the onyx stone. And the name of the second river is Gihon: the same is it that compasseth the whole land of Ethiopia. And the name of the third river is Hiddekel: that is it which goeth toward the east of Assyria. And the fourth river is Euphrates. And the Lord God took the man, and put him into the garden of Eden to dress it and to keep it. And the Lord God commanded the man, saying, Of every tree of the garden thou mayest freely eat; but of the tree of the knowledge of good and evil, thou shalt not eat of it: for in the day that thou eatest thereof thou shalt surely die. And the Lord God said, It is not good that the man should be alone; I will make him an help meet for him. And out of the ground the Lord God formed every beast of the field, and every fowl of the air; and brought them unto Adam to see what he would call them; and whatsoever Adam called every living creature, that was the name thereof. And Adam gave names to all cattle, and to the fowl of the air, and to every beast of the field; but for Adam there was not found an help meet for him. And the Lord God caused a deep sleep to fall upon Adam, and he slept: and he took one of his ribs, and closed up the flesh instead thereof; and the rib, which the Lord God had taken from man, made he a woman, and brought her unto the man.　And Adam said, This is now bone of my bones, and flesh of my flesh: she shall be called Woman, because she was taken out of Man.　Therefore shall a man leave his father and his mother, and shall cleave unto his wife: and they shall be one flesh. And they were both naked, the man and his wife, and were not ashamed.—*Genesis 2:8-25*.

Let us from the very beginning bear in mind that the story of paradise, as every Bible story, is written very distinctly for men of today.　It desires to tell us something for our daily life as we must live it today.　Preposterous!　Impossible!　I hear you object.　Is not this story particularly remote from us and foreign to our life?　What has the garden of Eden with its trees and streams and the story of the first human pair in common with what we call "our life"?　What point of contact has it with present-day events and interests, or with the thoughts that fill our minds, or with the cares and tasks from which we come and which will soon again claim our attention?　Is not ours an entirely different world?

The more actively we are engaged in the many affairs of life the more keenly do we seem to feel that the story of paradise is really out of date.　On the contrary, I would answer, the more concrete and real our interest in life as we must live it the better we shall understand this story.　Our homes and streets, our offices and factories and shops are the places where this story belongs.　There, and there alone, can we really hear

what it says. It is a story for men who are surrounded
and entrapped by the many problems and enigmas of
life.

Think, then, of that part of actual life which happens
to be your portion! Think of yourself! Of your good
points, yes; but think even more of your weaknesses!
Think of those things of which you do not like to remind yourself or be reminded! Openly or secretly,
they make up the larger part of your life anyway.
Think of your faults and failures then, and of the difficult times through which you must pass! Think of
your wife, who walks by your side that you should not
be alone—if you are a man! And if you are a wife,
think of the husband whose helpmeet you are called to
be! Think of your children, these remarkable images
of yours! Think of the future, if you are young; and
if you are old, recall what lies behind you! Think of
death slowly but surely coming to meet you! Or, let us
just think of tomorrow, of next week, or the next hour
and all that is waiting for us at home! Think of the
larger questions and problems besetting our country and
our age, if you will! And now, in the midst of all—
the story of paradise? What does it mean? What will
it tell us?

It tells us something altogether strange and foreign,
a story that is beautiful and another that is terrible. Its
beautiful tale tells us that the life which we are now
living is not our first and last, not our only, life. How
shall I express it? Before and behind our life there

was, and is, and always will be, another life, an altogether different life: our life in the origin. At bottom, it is our true life even until today. Its dreadful tale tells us that we can never, never again, return to this our true and genuine life. It speaks to us of a fathomless depth which separates us irrevocably from our yonder life; and neither dreams nor yearnings will transport us across the yawning abyss.

Irrevocably and irrefutably we are told: No, you are no longer men in paradise; you are living in a hard and cold world and age. The story of paradise does not call us away from the actuality of our life, as poets transport us into a land of dreams and make-believe. It does not indicate ways of escape from hard and cold facts to a so-called better life. On the contrary, it cuts off our flight into unreality by telling us that paradise is irrevocably lost to us. It discovers this fact for us as it shows us the boundary which bars us from the land which we have lost.

As a prisoner becomes fully aware where and what he is only when the prison keeper enters his cell, so the story of paradise makes us fully conscious that we have lost God's destiny for us. It is and remains a word of judgment and severest condemnation. Surely, it does not invite futile dreams. Much rather, it opens our eyes to what we should be but are not. It makes us restless and dissatisfied with our present world and life. We shall never be at home here. All the days of our life we shall be homesick for the life which we have lost. We have here no abiding city; we are but guests and pilgrims here below. Yes, the loss of our home, which makes us strangers and wanderers, is the real mark of our humanity. It is the one characteristic common to all of us. It is the hidden root from which spring forth our restlessness and our every question. It is the central point of our life around which circle, secretly or openly, all our thoughts.

A dreadful story, yes; but is it a strange tale? Would you say it is untrue to life, foreign to us? Would you say it does not concern us? Are we not in fact guests and pilgrims? Does not every day that comes and goes tell us that? Is it not the truest story of our life? Does it not uncover what at bottom we know only too well? Is not this the strongest bond of human fellowship even if we do not care to admit it?

But let us listen on! What is that home that we all have lost but from which we all have come as surely as we live and while we live? We call it "paradise." Perhaps it is not a good name. It is likely to make us think of a poet's dream-world which has no existence in reality. The story of the garden of Eden and the first man there tells us of a world which we have lost, to be sure; but it is a real world nevertheless. However strange it may sound to our ears, it speaks of it quite soberly and distinctly as of a real and tangible place. To be sure—let us remember the chasm separating us from it!—it is not a place that we know and can seek and find. It does not lie within the realm which is subject to our discoveries. It lies beyond our nature and history. To say it once again, it lies before, and behind, and beyond us.

When the history of man began; when man's time had its beginning; when time and history commenced where man has the first and the last word, paradise had disappeared. For it is peculiar to our lost home that God, and not man, is the Lord. God is all, and He has the first and last word there. Yet, let us erase every picture and color with which not the Bible but our own phantasy has adorned paradise. Let us have ears only for what the Bible says again and again, once, twice, four times, six times: And the Lord God planted . . . ; and the Lord God made to grow . . . ; and the Lord God took . . . ; and the Lord God commanded . . . ; and the Lord God said. . . . . There, and there alone, is paradise where the Lord God is the One central point from whom everything has its beginning and in whom everything has its life. God is Lord! God is king! God is! God takes! God gives! Do you hear this steady hammer-beat of the story? God is the Lord, and man and the earth and all its creatures are subject to him.

Nothing, nothing disturbs the happy play of the creature before its Creator. Beautiful harmony of all beings with their origin is the simple content of this story. Can we think out its reality and its meaning? We cannot! Oh, we cannot, for we have lost paradise! Do you understand our tragedy? Here is the misery and burden which weigh so heavily upon our life. Here is the dark and dreary shadow that lies like a somber pall over our earth, over all nature and history. We have trifled away what God's goodness designed for us in the beginning.

But let us listen on! The Bible knows what we no longer know. If we look closely, the story of paradise does not portray a perfect state. It does not paint dreamland for us as it relates the life of the first man. Again, it speaks of the simple actuality of man's world. It describes the earth, the earth with its trees and animals, and man, the actual man. It is all so familiar to us, is it not? Let us attend only to this, that this first man in paradise receives a command. He may eat of all the trees in the garden, but of one tree he must not eat on pain of death.

He is not a blessed spirit living in absolute perfection. Under circumstances he can sin and die. But what is important and decisive is this, that he is not under necessity to sin and therefore he must not necessarily die. On the contrary—and here we are made to face again the glory of the life which we have lost—man can obey God. He can do what we are no longer able to do: he can avoid sin. And therefore he can also live, really and truly live, live a life which alone deserves to be called life, for the pall of death does not lie over it. For God is there the Lord. In letters large and clear we see it written: The Lord God.

Truly, it is *our* life which the story of paradise portrays, but it is our life lived in full harmony with God.

Because it is lived in the presence of God it is so altogether different from what we call and know as our life. It is, in fact, so different that our life is really not life at all in view of this vital life which man received at the beginning from the hands of God. Sin and death are the shackles of our present life. They are clamped on us and throttle us and invert its meaning. But there they are missing.

Have you no use for the story which transcends our comprehension? There is for man a possibility to live without the fearful necessity which is upon all of us; there is a life without the necessity of sin and death. Where man really lives in the presence of God; where God can be for us what He would like to be for us, Creator and Father; where man is what he should be, a child that lives in obedience to His Father, there such a life is possible.

We can no longer fathom what it means to be free from compulsion to sin. *We* must sin! Day by day and hour after hour we do what we ought not to be doing and what we would not do, but nevertheless do, because we cannot do otherwise. We are prisoners. Who is there among us who does not know something of our inability to keep from doing what we should not do? Who does not suffer under it? Who does not know of hours when we can only feel deeply, deeply ashamed of ourselves because we are what we are? And now the story of paradise tells us, it must not be necessarily so.

Adam and Eve were not ashamed. There is a possi-

9527

bility—in God—that we do not have to sin. And this incomprehensible possibility is *our* possibility; but now a deep chasm bars us from it. Can we deny that the story speaks the truth? Are we not ashamed of ourselves because we know that if *God* were in our life as He wanted to be in the beginning we should be free, free from sin and shame? If—yes, if! But now it is certain that we must sin. And we must die!

Irrevocably we all are moving toward the moment when our present life which is not life comes to a close. Who does not at least suspect that it comes to an end because it never was real life? For how should it then come to an end? But why is it not real life? Is it God's fault? Did He bungle when He created us and gave us life? Or are *we* perhaps at fault? Does perhaps our guilt come to the light of day at death? If so, who is not afraid of his hour of death? And once again, the story of paradise tells us that it need not be so.

Death would not need to be death. Guided by the hand of God, who is our Creator and Father, we could make blessed progress from one degree of perfection to another. It could be so! Death, as we know it now, was not originally in the Creator's plan. It is not a part of humanity's God-given constitution. Death is guilt; *our* guilt! We could—from God—be free from guilt and free from death, *if* . . . , yes, *if* . . . !

Let us also consider a third fact in the story of paradise. See the marvelous simplicity and beautiful transparency of the relation and order between man and

woman. We know how sin, which is our disobedience
against the ordinances of God, finds its chief bulwark
here. There have been men and women who have pro-
tested under the fearful pressure of these things. Oh
that there were no such thing as being husband or wife
with its terrible load of pains and sorrows! No, says
the Bible, sexes may be; it is not an unclean thing from
the beginning. The Lord God created them pure, man
and wife. He really meant to do right and be gracious
when he did not leave man alone, but gave him woman
as his helpmeet. If He is in the midst, then this sphere
of our existence over which large promises are inscribed
but over which now lie deep shadows can become light
and full of blessedness. If . . . !

Do we now understand a little that this Bible story
concerns us deeply, very deeply indeed? Does it not
apply very directly to our life? Does it not discover
our deepest sorrow, our most secret misery? Truly, *I*
am the man who is meant! I should be living a different life, a life wholly different from the one I am
living; for *I* have my origin from God. He did not
create me for sin and death, but for His vital life. It is
true what is written here. And truly, it is written not
only here. Far from the Bible all the deeper spirits of
humanity have divined and said that our present life
is not our only life; it is not our true life.

There is a life which is not froth and dream. Another
life is our real destiny. But one thing these thinkers
without the Bible did not see nor consider: the deep

chasm which separates us from this divine life. We shall, we can reach it if . . . ! But this "shall" and "can" are long since lost. And what these men think and say of this new and different life which is destined for us is therefore in reality only froth and dream. It would therefore be quite foolish if I were to exhort you now: Go and seek the true life! Strive to obtain it; see how you may enter into harmony with the Infinite! Excelsior! You may tell a prisoner, Be free! He ought to be free, he could be free, if, yes, if he had not trifled away his freedom, if the prison gate had not been locked behind him. He could be free, yes; but in reality he is not free at all to become free.

But something else I am permitted to say before I close. Why does the Bible tell us this grave story of paradise? Is it really only for the purpose of telling us where and what we should be if the door had not been shut between God and men? Does it not tell it to us because in it and with it God visits us in our prison that He may speak to us? To speak to us in our prison about our prison? And if this is true—and it is true—if God himself speaks out of this story to us who are separated from Him, are we then still separated from Him?

Must we not ask the breath-taking question, If God addresses us, addresses us with severity and judgment, but after all addresses us, what else can it be but—paradise? No, not immediately paradise, but grace! Grace and again grace for men who have trifled away paradise, who have become guilty before Him. But, marvel of marvels, God in His mercy does not forsake them! And lest it remain a question whether there is grace, grace for men who are compelled to wander far from home in sin and death, God has not only given us this Old Testament story of paradise. No, He has given us another word, His last and His own peculiar word: Jesus Christ.

Truly, into the very midst of our prison, into the very midst of our wanderings, into the very midst of our sin and death, He came, the Son of the Father full of grace and truth. And now? Will sin and death now cease? No, but there is a way, a marvelous and incomprehensible way through the very midst of sin and death; a path for us prisoners; a way for us mortals on which the Father is with us. Now we are not in paradise, to be sure. We are in this world of ours. But we may know, as truly as that first man in paradise, God is here. And it cannot be otherwise than that the atmosphere from paradise will fill our prison cells.

The deep chasm is still here; but He who is the Lord comes to us across the deep abyss and we learn to walk by His hand. We are pilgrims; but we know— no, we are not dreaming!—we know of a home that is waiting to receive us. We suffer and die, but we have a great hope. We have earthly thoughts, but in their very midst something that is truer than all earthiness flashes up. We are at no other place than at the very one at which we are and live. We shall go home to our cares, and probably to our sins. But He also is here;

He goes along, and because He goes along we shall not despair. For with Him comes forgiveness, comes victory. We are lonely; we are selfish; but we know the Creator of our life, and how should we now fail to recognize the end which He has set to our ungraciousness? How should we fail finally, finally to recognize the brother and neighbor whom He has given us that we might be delivered from the vain service and slavery of our selfish nature?

But is it true? May we say such great things of us who are so small and sinful and subject to death? We do not say it easily. We do not make this claim on our own authority. But must we not say them? May we keep silence, since God has visited us in our prison? What we say we say to the praise of His mighty grace and not to praise ourselves. We cannot escape its constraint, since His word is here. We must hear it. Therefore we also speak. Oh that we would hear it, really hear it! Then we should also live, truly and really live.

In the midst of all the sham and fraud of this vain life a trace of eternal life would then appear among us! In the midst of our darkness a ray of God's glory would then become visible. We all are thirsting for this life. Let us go to the fountain! Let us hear and heed His word; for He says: Let him that thirsteth come unto me and drink!

IX.

THE BEGINNING FROM ABOVE

Having then a great high priest, who hath passed through the heavens, Jesus the Son of God, let us hold fast our confession. For we have not a high priest that cannot be touched with the feeling of our infirmities; but one that hath been in all points tempted like as we are, yet without sin. Let us therefore draw near with boldness unto the throne of grace, that we may receive mercy, and may find grace to help us in time of need.—*Hebrews 4:14-16*.

Ascension Day! Jesus Christ ascended into heaven and sitteth at the right hand of the Father, from whence He shall come to judge the quick and the dead. If what we commemorate today is true, it is meet, however new and strange it appears, that our text begins in so extraordinary a manner from above and links us up immediately with God—"having then" (since we have)—in order to comfort us, as those who already have, with an assurance of mercy and grace, and to exhort us: "Let us hold fast our confession" and "Let us therefore draw near."

What shall we say? Do not the words "we *have*" startle us? Are they not at best true as the result and goal of much meditation and speculation, of many experiences and intensest labors? Is it not necessary to begin with a discussion of our human problems, doubts and frailties?   Should we not, after an evaluation of possible ways of escape from our misery, proceed to expound the good and royal way which leads us to the goal and finally close with a description of the goal, with itself, what we have and what it means to us?   This compellingly forceful new beginning from above may indeed startle us.   But there is perhaps some little readiness on our part not to resist it completely.

We may have a little understanding that when God speaks to men He must begin as He does—from above! Perhaps we have too often made the attempt in our own life and in our dealings with others to work our own way to the heights out of the depths of our human problems, cares and afflictions.   Perhaps we have too often heard men speak, as men are wont to speak, of man's ways to the heights.   Full of good will, but with little or no understanding, they sought to give counsel and encouragement.   Perhaps the remembrance of their appeals is not altogether pleasant.   They tired us.   We were not always certain but that some beautiful though dangerous illusions were being brought into play to dazzle and beguile us.   Perhaps it dawned on us that the ways of men will not do; that, in fact, they must not succeed.

They do not bring real help; on the contrary, they result in deeper injury and greater damage.   Perhaps our minds are for this reason not entirely closed when we are told that as certainly as it is true that Jesus Christ ascended into heaven, so certainly the word of God must speak to us in a manner different from the manner of men. It must make the astounding new beginning from above which it does make. But whether we are open minded or not, and whether we like it or not, the word of God differs from the words of men in this, that it does make its new beginning with us from above; yes, from a height beyond every height which we may choose for our goal.

"Having then a great high priest!" Are you listening? Because we have Him! For a beginning, let this be more important, infinitely more important than all your problems and difficulties; more important also than whatever answers and solutions to your questions men may offer you. You can really afford to be indifferent to any glorious goal which the world may set forth for you! You can afford to ignore the highways which are to lead you there! Instead of all these, begin now to say simply and as a child says, *"We have!"* How can I? you ask. How will I reach it? And I answer: You can do nothing toward it, and you will never reach it. Do you not hear *"We have"*? You are not told we have somehow won or acquired or earned it. We are only told *"We have!"* We are not told that in one way or another we have reached our high destiny; but we, even you and I, are already there, and from this height the road will lead us down the hill rather than uphill. In this manner the word of God makes its new beginning from above.

Surely no man may make such a beginning with us. Not even the Bible would dare to do so if it were merely an exposition of the wisdom of men. No sermon would dare to make such a start with us if preaching were merely training in the wisdom of men. The word of God alone dares to make this beginning with us; and it does so in fact. You ask perhaps if it is indifferent to the needs and problems of men. Assuredly not! You will hear it speak of compassion with our infirmities, of mercy and grace which we shall find. Would to God the wisdom of men were even remotely as sympathetic to the needs of men as is the word of God! But the word of God desires to begin with itself; it wants to make a new beginning from above. From there it will not deny us illumination and help in our every care.

If only we are obedient, it will abundantly bless us. You ask if it does not give commands, directions and counsels? Certainly, it does! Listen to these: "Let us hold fast our confession!" "Let us draw near with boldness!" Are not these appeals and exhortations enough? Shall we be done with them so quickly that we have reason to complain that challenges are wanting? It is true that the exhortation of the word of God differs from the varieties of human appeals. There is most certainly no dearth of them; for it is not given until what is decisive has come to pass. It says: Take heed; the decision in your favor has already been cast. Let it stand as having taken place! Acknowledgment

is all that is required of you.　Acknowledge it!　Is not
this perhaps the reason that the many words of admonition and consolation which resound in our world are
so asthmatic and so devoid of fruit because they are
launched from a false start?　These hollow comforters
and exhorters do not dare to presuppose that a decision
in our favor has already been made.　Their comfort
and exhortation do not start from above, as does the
word of God when it says: *"Since we have!"*

My friends, our eyes are at first almost blinded by
the dazzling splendor of this bold beginning from
above: We have!　But if the word of God is true,
though incomprehensible, it can mean nothing else than
that a real new beginning has been made for us above.
It is a fact, then, that we are already with God, and
everything that we think we should and can bring in
order will be brought in order from there.　But how?
Is it perhaps because we are of divine origin?　Because
somehow or somewhere our heavenly origin lies im-
bedded in our own soul, so that we merely need to
plumb its depth in order to give our assent to this bold
saying of the word of God, "We have"?　Would that
mean holding fast our confession?　Sometimes we hear
it so interpreted.　But I fear that we have forgotten
that though we are indeed of divine origin we have
trifled away our connection with our origin and lost it.

I fear we are overlooking the patent fact that our
daily life is a denial of our divine origin.　In a maze
of fanciful dreams we have then forgotten our actuality

a little. If we think of a divine sanctuary in our hearts when we say "We have," our hands are empty. "We have" has then dissolved into thin air. A little honesty on our part will convince us quickly. Neither do we need to look for this beginning from above in this, that we have turned about face and reconquered our lost home, or at least a small part of it. We are sometimes told that "drawing near with boldness" means to turn about face and reconquer what we have lost until victory is complete. But would it not be better to stay honestly with the questions we have already asked: How can I? How shall I succeed?

The confession "We have" can never be full of joy and assurance if it is founded on our conquest of the kingdom of heaven! Pray, when did we ever turn face about in its direction? Where is the mountain which we can boast to have climbed successfully? Do not such illusions vanish as the snow before the spring-time sun in the very moment when we give a little serious thought to the question whether we hope to die in peace on the strength of our feeble attempts to regain the kingdom of heaven? Do we really expect to make any kind of showing with them before God's judgment seat? No, if the word of God speaks of a new beginning from above which has been made for us it does not speak of a divine nature immanent in us or acquired by us. *"We have,"* so we are told, *"a great high priest, Jesus, the Son of God who has passed through the heavens!"* What does it mean? At any rate this, that *we have another who has made a new beginning from above for us.* Let us consider the several thoughts in due order.

We have *another!* My friends, here you have the heart and kernel of the word of God. It is the key to the fact that we are really a people for whom another, a high priest, Jesus Christ, had to make, and did make, the new beginning from above. Such a beginning had to be made if our human problems and errors, our transgressions and sufferings, are to be attacked at the root, and if our confession "We have" is to be really full of joy and assurance. We shall joyously and honestly exclaim "We have!" only if we can continue: "We have a great high priest! We have another! We have Jesus, the Son of God, who has passed through the heavens;" *We* are not Jesus, the Son of God! Here we can only say "Lord, go out from me; for I am a sinful man!" And then? Thanks be to God, who has given us the victory through our Lord Jesus Christ!

Two things are done to us when the word of God tells us that we have another. When it sets forth openly, as Paul once said, before our eyes Jesus Christ our high priest, we are at first thoroughly humbled. We are told that it is not a weak confession of human impotence or slothfulness, but God's truth, if we see and confess that no road of our own, however eagerly we shall seek and choose it, will lead us to the heights. It is God's truth that we are and shall remain in the lowlands, even if our goodwill were ten times

better than it is. We shall not lift ourselves by our
own bootstraps out of the mire. It is God's truth that
another must intercede for us—and has interceded for
us! Is it not something like a dethronement for us if
we are bidden to look to another, to a high priest?

But the same word of God which humbles us also
makes us free. It frees us from the torture of making
good where we are not able to make good. It frees us
of futile dreams and bitter awakenings which are ever
and inevitably a part of our undertakings. It frees us
of the untempered hardness with which men, the would-
be saints and the sinners, are wont to deal with each
other on their ways to the heights. But it does not
only free us of these things; it also makes room for a
simple and wholehearted trust; for unpretentious
obedience; for a real love of the neighbor which is
real in this that it does not remonstrate because it sees
no reason for remonstrating. For all these the word
of God makes us free. See here the new beginning
from above: Let yourself be humbled and made free!
Let the truth that Jesus Christ, the Other One, intercedes for you and stands in God's presence for you
break you and make you whole! So, and therefore,
it is true that you are truly with God, whom you shall
never succeed in finding on your own road to the
heights.

For this is what He does: He intercedes for us. *He
makes a new beginning for us from above.* Without
Him our own beginnings are retrogression. De-

termined from eternity, His high-priestly service is done for all eternity. What does the high priest do whom the word of God sets forth? Very simply this: He is in the presence of God such a man as God, for the sake of His truth and holiness, insists on having with Him. But we ourselves do not at all care to be such men. For He *carries* the sin of the world, while we deny and condemn it as we accuse and blame others. He acknowledges as just the punishment which lies as God's wrath on every man, while we minimize as much as possible our own part in it; and hide from ourselves and others that we are lost. He *suffers* and does not seek to evade suffering. Thus He stands before our eyes at the climax of His life, in His death on the cross. So He took the life of men absolutely serious in the sight of God.

In order to do this simple thing He had to be God's own Son. For it is patent that we do not want to do this simple thing. We refuse, and our refusal is the constant renewal of our sin. Thus, with His activity, He has reconciled us to God. So He spoke the word which is at the same time a proclamation of God's kingdom and our acquittal. Not we: He! His absolute otherness is shown in this, that He does the simple thing which we refuse to do. He has done it, once and for all. The word is spoken and it is now in force. He arose and ascended into heaven; it means that His word is spoken for all eternity. It is spoken from heaven: God himself has spoken it. Yesterday, today, and in all eternity, Jesus Christ stands between God and us, Himself God and Himself man.   Among us the Divine.

He is as one of us with God, possessing and executing with power His will to let His good deed be our deed and taking our evil deed upon Himself as if it were His.   Therefore, and so, He does not attack our human misery in its twigs and branches, but at the very root. Therefore a throne of grace is here established to which we may draw near with boldness, as our text says, in order to receive grace and mercy to help us in time of need; yes, in the day when our eyes are really opened to the fact that we cannot help ourselves—and we do not have to wait for the hour of our death!—in the day when we know that in all upward movements of our own we are really only going around in circles and walking on one spot.   They will never remove us from the judgment in which we stand.   He who intercedes for us is Jesus Christ, our high priest.   This is the new beginning from above which has been made for us.

We *have*, however, this high priest.   Oh, methinks we now understand that we have Him because He has us.   For this reason our having is so joyous and so sure, because it cannot be anything else than an ever new understanding and apprehension of this unfathomable truth: He has us!   But now our text says of this understanding something that is very comforting and severe.   It says it very emphatically in order to remind us also from this angle of the new beginning from above.   We hear: "We have not a high priest that cannot be touched with the feeling of our infirmities; but one that hath been in all points tempted like as we are, yet without sin." What does it mean? Certainly this, that we neither must, nor dare, have Him separated from our actual life.

In our infirmities, in a life that is endangered by temptations on all sides, we shall have Him. Let us not think that we must first rise to some secure and safe height of purity and power in order to have Him. Let us not think that we must occupy a place where we can stand without blushing before men. Men indeed are without mercy. Among men we have to be afraid if we let them see the fears which fill our hearts, though at bottom there is none without them. Let us not discuss whether it is even humanly advisable to play at such a comedy where we appear in a role of happiness and assurance when our heart and conscience are far from them.

Be not deceived! From such a place we have no access to Christ. We are merely throwing up a barricade on our only way to Him. We *may* and we *shall* come to Christ as we are; as we actually are. And in life we are really not the little gods to whom life is so simply meaningful and to whom joy and kindness come easy. We may succeed in playing such a part for a season. Our actuality, however, is our infirmity and our susceptibility to temptation. Arrogance now and now melancholy; now effeminate vanity, now callous uncharitableness; now thoughtless folly, now useless

grovelings; now despair of God, now wicked stubbornness against His well-known will endanger us. This
is man; such creatures we are—unsecured against a
host of foes. Who will contradict?

And now we are not to evade this actuality of ours
if we would understand and apprehend Jesus Christ
who is risen and ascended into heaven as the One who
has made a new beginning for us from above. If we
run away from our infirmities we deny this "from
above" with our would-be affirmation of Jesus Christ.
He has compassion on us as we are. He has identified
Himself with us as we are. To such as we are in reality
He is near. In the condition in which we are He says
His great word: I for you! Your sin shall be mine
and my divine grace shall be for you! How can it fail
to be gospel, glad tidings, that we have such an high
priest who receiveth sinners and eateth with them! For
who does not know that he is sitting at such a sinner's
table too? There, there God must find us, whether
we like it or not, if He is to find us at all!

But how can we fail to be terrified to have such a
high priest who passes us by while we are secure in ourselves and who waits until He finds us really, honestly
at this table?

Let us hold fast our confession! Let us draw near
with boldness! To confess and to draw near means
that we acknowledge the new beginning from above
as having been made. Perhaps we have a feeling that
we are hearing what we have only waited to hear and

accept.   Is it, however, not true that we know also that
we can only pray, beseech and cry out, Come, Creator
Spirit!   Lord, have compassion on us! lest we should
have heard in vain.   And if we have not heard in vain
we can only praise and give thanks: Lord God, thou
hast opened the ears of one who was deaf.   Because it
is grace to draw near to the throne of grace, it is done,
when it is done, with boldness!

X.

HOSANNA, HELP!

And Jesus entered into the temple of God, and cast out all them that sold and bought in the temple, and overthrew the tables of the money-changers, and the seats of them that sold the doves; and he saith unto them, It is written, My house shall be called a house of prayer: but ye make it a den of robbers. And the blind and the lame came to him in the temple; and he healed them. But when the chief priests and the scribes saw the wonderful things that he did, and the children that were crying in the temple and saying, Hosanna to the son of David; they were moved with indignation, and said unto him, Hearest thou not what these are saying? And Jesus saith unto them, Yea; did ye never read, Out of the mouth of babes and sucklings thou hast perfected praise?

—Matthew 21:12-16.

In the center of this powerful story is the wrath and the fury with which Jesus, storming, forcibly cleansed the temple. There are also the traders, the bourgeois and the shopkeepers, over whose heads it is written: "Out with you!" There also stand the scribes, the theologians and their following, the leaders of the people in politics and church, the tenfold clever men with their feigned indignation, who, for once, at least for a moment, have found their master and have to keep still. There also stand the lame and the blind, who know

119

nothing else to do but to beg, beg every day, to get their bit of bread in the temple, and who now have this chance to beg taken away, being no longer lame and blind, for "He healed them."

There stand also those few babes and children who can contain themselves no longer and whose mouths are opened almost against their will, we might say. They can do nothing else. They must shout, as a child will, shout in spite of everything: "Hosanna to the Son of David!"

That is what is really the touching, stirring, and unforgetable thing about this temple narrative. It is the shouting of the children, there in the very citadel of the enemy, in the midst of the temple. It is a singular moment we are facing. Jesus is going toward His cross; it is the beginning of His passion. His way becomes narrow and steep; the walls of His suffering rise high before Him. He will be delivered up for judgment, condemned to death, sentenced, mocked, rejected. The world, yes, the world of men whom He had loved so much, thrust Him out. Blood and tears await Him. And there, before all this breaks in upon Him, we find this little band of babes and children, preparing for Him what others owe and deny Him.

They prepare for Him, in the eleventh hour, the praise of God of which He once said wistfully, and with burning heart, that He was come on earth to kindle a fire, and "How would I that it might already burn!" This praise of God from men for which He had striven, for which He will strive, and upon which He waits as upon nothing else, this praise comes to Him from babes and children which the great, the prudent, the secure, and the wise will not offer Him. Those who shouted "Hosanna to the Son of God!" were wretched creatures. And we all know, humanly speaking, that it no longer availed any. With the praise which they brought the Lord unwittingly they could not save Him from that terrible road which He must walk. They themselves hardly knew what they shouted as they cried "Hosanna to the Son of David!" And yet it is like a last greeting to Him from this world that thrusts Him into suffering. It seems as if these desperately crying children would tell Him, "You have not been here entirely in vain; you do not go to your death in vain; we have not understood you and yet we have understood; our ears have been closed and yet we have heard. Accept our weak praise on earth, take it, let it be pleasing unto you, do not reject us. Hosanna, help us!"

And He—He did not reject the praise of these children and babes; it did not go past Him; He heard the voice of these babes; He accepted it and it did Him good and He would not tolerate it when they tried to silence them. Of course, in itself this shouting of the street urchins in the temple did not amount to so much. But because He accepted it, it became praise unto God which should not be wanting in this hour. And so it came to pass, because He accepted this shouting of the children and babes as praise to God, that this shouting has never quite ceased. It has gone on and on. Again and again it broke out; it appeared again and again in the midst of the history of Christianity right in the Church.

I could almost say that this shouting is the essential, the abiding thing, the substance of the history of the Church through all the centuries, which recurred again and again, and which broke out again and again. One could understand the entire history of the Church from this angle. Two streams run through it. There is the stream of external history of organized Christianity, of these princes and politicians of the Church, the bishops and their theologians with their systems; there are the councils and conferences where Church history is made externally. And it is always true of all of them that Jesus Christ was not understood and that He was thrust aside by them, delivered up and crucified. But thanks and praise be to God, there is always a hidden undercurrent beside and behind the official course of events, alongside of and behind the loud noise of the official world history and Church history.

Here a few, there a few of these babes, a few little folks, a few foolish ones—their eyes are opened and they recognize something of the greatness and the power of the Saviour, though not because of any merit on their part. And because this has dawned upon them, they must shout; it must out; they cannot keep it to themselves! Men threaten them and try to silence them, but without success. The cry of these babes and children simply goes on and becomes praise to God, seemingly lost and heard by no one, drowned in the howling of the storm which roars through our times, and yet not lost. For again and again it happens that out of this hidden undercurrent and from these children and babes this shouting rises up and breaks into the great Church and its history, and these are the truly significant moments of the history of the Church.

Such a babe and foolish one, warned a hundred times to stick to the rule, and yet never to be silenced, was Martin Luther, that "monklet" who sat there in Wittenberg in his cell back of his Bible and read: It is written! He got up and had to cry out, shout out something of what he had read. And God heard this cry and through Luther interfered mightily into the great history of the Church and the history of the world.

Such a small, insignificant, foolish "babe of a man" was that Christopher Blumhardt, who in the nineteenth century discovered something of the triumphal story of Jesus Christ on earth in his obscure Suabian village and had to shout out something in spite of, and to the chagrin of, the theologians and "scribes" of his time. God heard this cry and accepted it. And it has become a praise to God even in our day. But we may think of ourselves, too. We may think of all of that weak, truly unintelligible, humble seeking and groping for the way of God as it lives in us, hidden, covered, choked up. We may think about our own faint surmising and conception of what Christ Jesus is to us. We may think of all our poor attempts to give Him a little honor in our lives, to serve Him, to follow Him, to belong to Him. As out of a deep subterranean vault something in us cries out for a God who helps.

Let us think about the mystery of Jesus Christ as it rises up before the eyes of innumerable people today, even before the eyes of the heathen peoples out there in Africa and Asia. There they are, these babes, children, sucklings, as the Bible states, in whom something is beginning to cry out. It might be that in their cry inheres the praise of God, and that this is the true fruit of the Kingdom of Heaven in our day, this hidden groping and seeking after Him and His help alone.

It will always be thus, that there is something in us which is at first quite different from this hosanna-crying, out of which God could prepare His praise. There is, first of all, the world, with its noise and its sorrow. And we are full of this world. In us is worry, indifference and apostasy from God. We forget God. Who cares about His commandments or His way? Do we not all go our own way, do we not all seek our own thoughts and make our own plans? But in the midst of this rebellion against God there is of a sudden that groping for God's hands from which we simply cannot desist. Or there is perhaps in secret a man, a woman, a human being who feels he must kneel down and entreat God: Hosanna, do help! Perhaps a man has developed for himself a view of life, an outlook on the world, and now questions are assailing him upon all sides. He is almost rent in pieces by his problems. But in the midst of it all, quite beyond his understanding and yet present in him, is the memory of the God who does not forsake the doubter. Perhaps there is in these days and weeks a youth preparing for confirmation or Church membership, who has certainly not understood very much about the great truth of God, which has been explained to him out of the Bible, but who has understood so much as to see clearly: "He, God, must walk with me; I do not understand Him, but I know I am in His hands and He leads me so that it will be well with my life." That is praise to God, prepared out of the mouths of babes and children.

Perhaps we ourselves are living in such a remarkable moment where we know something of the guilt there is in our lives. We have long tried to say there is no God. Now we know it is a lie. God lives and I am in His hands. And what will become of me in the grasp of His hands? And we can no longer do otherwise, we must go to Him and confess our sins. *He* must forgive them. If he does not forgive we shall be lost. That is praise to God, prepared for Him out of the mouths of sinners and dying men.

There will always be pharisees and scribes standing by who will try to spoil our praying and shouting for us. Perhaps there are people very near to us who cannot comprehend it that we are of a sudden bearing like a light in our hands the praise to God that has been prepared through our lives. They handle us roughly; they cannot endure our praying or going to Church, nor that we no longer chime in with their bitter laments over these hard times and the wickedness of men; that we are a bit more confident and hopeful and that we seem to know about One Who helps us. But it may be that our wise and clever thoughts, or embitterment and care, raise their voices within us and say, "My, what are you thinking? God will leave you in the lurch anyway!"

Through all that we will have to cry "Hosanna to the Son of David!" We simply will not let anyone dissuade us from this new way upon which we have chanced to come, where one trusts God because he knows about Jesus Christ. So men praise God out of the depths. Thus one has his eyes opened for God who dwells in the heights, but also is with those of a bruised and humble heart.

It is an altogether remarkable, yes, a tremendous, moment 'twixt heaven and earth when things come to that point that the praise of God awakens in the babes and the humble. But it is then that we may do in imperfection and weakness and disgrace what the angels, the blessed and the perfect do in power and glory. In such moments we grant that God is right. The whole rule of God in our lives tends to bring us to that point where this happens: Not that it may go well with us, not that our way in life shall be smooth and easy, not that we shall be spared the storms and the temptations, but that in storms and temptations we may come to that point where praise to God breaks forth.

The praise of God!   A Russian poet has said that every tiny leaf on the trees is a praise to God.   And it is true.   The praise of God surrounds us human beings and flows all around us.   See the stars, the mountains, the blossoming trees, the flowers of summer, the fruit of the autumn.   All of this, as the apostle says, is a sign whereby one can recognize the power and the glory of God in His work.   And in the midst of all these creations which praise God stands man; and the same psalm that contains the word about the babes through whom God has prepared Himself praise, says about him (man) that he is the most glorious creation of God, a little lower than God himself.   This creature does not bring God his praise.

In the midst of the rejoicing of creation and in the midst of the rejoicing of the perfect, the blessed and the angels this creature called man (which we are) is silent.   What an enigma that God is thus hidden from us, as though there were a wall back of which we stand, not praising God nor seeing Him!   What an enigma, this incomprehensible rushing out of the Father's house into the world without a God, as did the prodigal son!   Can it go on like this?   Will it not come to pass that man will open his mouth and praise God?   How long will it last, and when will that happen?   That is *the* question.

With tense expectation, one might say, they look down from the eternal world upon this human being— will he come to the point where God will receive His praise from him? In this expectation the Son of God descended and He did what we do not do, for He—without us—but among us and for us—prepared God's praise for Him on earth. His whole life, the entire life of the Saviour, is not to be understood in any other way but that once a human life was lived which, in its perfect obedience, was one mighty praise to God the Father. And this life was lived and spent in suffering, clear into the deepest depths where we would think thanksgiving and praise would leave a person. Yes, even to the cross and death He descended and still praised God there.

This took place and God was well pleased with His praise which the Son prepared for Him in life and in death. Now this pleasure of the Father in the Son has been disseminated among us by the Son; the wall is rammed through, God's loving-kindness and mercy have again become visible to us in the Son. Can it be otherwise but that among us sinners and dying men, who do not praise God, at last, at last the new man will rise who will praise God? Can it be otherwise but that at last, at last the prodigal son will return home and give to the Father that which he has never given Him, praise and love? God must become great among men.

That is the powerful dynamic in the life of Jesus. Down into the depths He carried God's praise, so that from then on the Hosanna, the shouting and crying for their Helper, may break forth from those below, the miserable, the downtrodden, the godless, and ascend to the throne of God, Who will accept it as praise prepared for Him. There is something in this story of the temple of this spiritual dynamic and coming of the Son with power and faithfulness from above—a suggestion of the response of those whom He has called, down there in their ignorance and their separation from God. Jesus Christ is certainly not come in vain. God the Father was honored in His Son. To be drawn, forcibly submerged, into this spiritual movement and to be able to do nothing more than respond—because He has called, as we may, in weakness, out of the depths—*that* is rightly to understand and to follow Jesus.

Three things we must yet bring up. The praise of God according to our story originated in the temple. The temple is the place where God is to be sought. We must add immediately, "sought" in human fashion, and somehow that always means in the wrong way. That is why Jesus had to cleanse the temple. What was this *human falsity* about which He became so infuriated, as never before? In the act of seeking God, man sought himself—wasn't that it? Big as you please, entirely at his ease, man stood there in the temple and thought he was somebody with his religious and pious gestures. He prayed, sacrificed, but only to *conceal* himself before his God in his complete nakedness and guilt. He made an ambush for thieves and murderers out of the place where one should completely surrender to God.

Such a thing Jesus had to expose. He actually had to drag *man* forward, right in the temple, from out of his pious hiding-place. We can come before God only in that we admit what was covered in the temple with offerings and prayers: I am poor, naked, before Thee; I am utterly at Thy mercy and in Thy hand; I am guilty! Before God man must at least become perfectly humble. To seek God, certainly that is what is involved in all religions. But we seek God in that we realize this: *I* cannot *find* Him; I cannot honor Him, I cannot praise Him as *I should*. He must seek and find me; then I shall have what I need. He must raise me up, and take pity on me.

The shadow of a great humility must fall over us, so that we only stand afar off and dare not lift up our eyes, but smite our breast and say, "Lord, be merciful to me, a sinner!" Wherever that takes place in the temple, there the temple has again become a house of prayer. Then the praise of God has again broken forth from the little ones, the babes.

Furthermore: the lame and the blind have been healed in the temple. What else does that mean, but that there has been help; real, divine power has come into the field and has routed the demon of sickness and need. God is He before Whom we are humble (little), but among these humble ones (little ones), among His miserable ones and sinners He is the One Who is great, great and always at hand in healing and saving. Has that not been almost entirely forgotten in our temples and churches?

XI.

PRAYING ARIGHT

Turn us again, O Jehovah God of hosts;
Cause Thy face to shine, and we shall be saved.
—*Psalm 80:19.*

In this first sacred hour of the new year let the word of God instruct us to pray thus: "Lord God of hosts, turn us again, cause Thy face to shine; and we shall be saved." Surely, we have an ear for the deep groanings which permeate this prayer, and for the wholly large joy which underlies these groanings. The word of God would lead us to stand before God wholly sad and wholly glad. On this remarkable crossroads God must see us even now. Do you understand that such a prayer would be a good beginning of the new year? Do you understand that it would be an exceedingly large blessing and help to be standing where we are taught to pray thus?

For we would be standing in the truth. For this is the truth as it is accessible to men, namely, that we must groan, yea, cry out in the throes of a death from which there is no escape; but in the midst of our misery we cannot groan and cry out as those who are in despair or as men who are lost.   No, we groan and cry out in joyous gratitude and hope because the same strong hand which is hurting us upholds us also.   What hopes have you for the new year?   Perhaps you are not quite clear. But surely you hope for truth, do you not?   For then we shall be free and able to live our life, whatever our lot may be.

The truth alone can make us free, and we can live our true life only as we stand in the truth.   If we only would understand that our real place is the abyss of misery, and that in this very abyss "the dayspring from on high hath visited us," we would be truly free and our days would become filled with real life.   We are waiting for freedom.   From day to day we are waiting, and especially today when a new succession of days with their mysteries is standing so auspiciously before us. And we would be standing in order at the place where we belong, and were it only the corner which we know to be the little corner assigned to us.

It may be a place without a great deal of glory, but it would be a place also where we could stand with a measure of security, since it is our place.   In a strange and hostile world it would be our little corner.   Do you not yearn for such a place at the beginning of this new year?   But even our little corner can be a crossroads only where great joy is mixed with deep groanings. Neither the one nor the other will let go of us.   There, there we would have formed our true place.

But I would not tempt you.   We cannot put our-

selves in that place of blessedness.   Every time we have
tried it we have put ourselves in a false position.   We
cannot even stand in this place on our own feet.   Every
time we thought to see that "I, I am standing there"
we found ourselves standing somewhere else.   Out of
the Holy Spirit the man of Scriptures prayed, "Lord
God of hosts, turn us, cause Thy face to shine, and we
shall be saved."   It is God's free will and gift and mercy
if we may thus stand before Him.

Just because it would be the best beginning of the
new year and the finest good deed and help to be thus
standing before God, we need to know and confess that
we have neither deserved the place, nor can we merit
it.   We are not capable of it.   No one can take it of himself.   It must be given him from above.   Praying aright,
yes, praying aright in particular, is something for which
one needs to pray.   And if the word of God instructs us
in our text, we must heed it as a question of great
urgency.

Are we by God's grace such people as pray aright
out of the Holy Spirit out of whom this man of Scripture has spoken?   Would we, by God's grace, become
such people?   What other response can we make if we
have heard the question aright than offer a fervent
prayer, "Lord, give me what Thou commandest and
then command what Thou wilt."   How should another
but God Himself be able to give us the right and decisive answer?

Thus we are asked a first question: Do you need to

be saved? Those whom God's grace has led into the truth, and truth into liberty, and liberty into a right disposition—those who pray aright—are people who need to be made whole because they are ill. Are we such? We are here in a place where the physical misery of our brothers and sisters brings vividly to our eyes what it means to be ill. But the majority of us who are assembled here do not, at least not visibly, belong to those who are physically ill. And even those among us who are physically ill do not perhaps clearly perceive that their particular illness is only a sign of an illness about which every one of us is asked.

All of us, those who are ill no less than those who are well, may belong to those who are well and therefore not in need of a physician. It would not be a good thing for us! I say, it would not be a good thing for us not to be ill. It would not be a good thing for us to enter the new year with an easy and confident step, with a self-satisfied heart and a sense of our rights, confident of our place, carefree about the question what may become of us. It is not a good thing for us because we would assuredly not be among those who, with the man in Scripture, can only groan for deliverance. God's grace, which is with those who are ill, would not yet have found us.

But, perchance, our imaginary wellbeing—which is really not well being—is, fortunately for us, only illusion. Are we not all men? Are we not all somehow touched by the flaming sword of the cherubim who lock the gate of paradise against us because we all have somehow forfeited the right to live there? When you counted yourself among those who are well, had you perhaps only forgotten or concealed the wound which you bear? Forgotten the burden which lies on you? Forgotten the perplexity which is troubling you? Yes, and if you do feel snug and safe, if perchance you consider yourself without guilt or care, can you maintain it even for a moment in view of these brothers and sisters here who belong to your body as surely as you belong to your own life?

See here the sufferers beside you! Are you really well while these are ill? Think of the underprivileged without number! If you have privileges, what right have you to them? Think of the host of those who have celebrated new year again in a wild and dissolute manner! Do you really think that you are safe on your decent, quiet and perhaps pious way? Or have you no part in their sin? Think of the many stubborn and headstrong brothers and sisters out there for whom the name "Christian" has become a name to be hated and scorned. You bear that name with joy and gratitude! Yes, but are you free of the godlessness which has broken out in these other members of the body of Christ? For that is what they are, after all! Are you really well? Will you still say that you are well? O you poor icicle of a Christian, if that were true!

But, after all, it is not true. Much rather it is true that we are all suffering from life's misery. It has so many names. It may be misery of our own or of another; it may be our common misery. It is here, at any rate. We are all crying out for salvation, because somewhere we are sorely pressed. There is none who is not on a sickbed. Let it be true, also for you! Believe it! It is God's healing grace if life's misery meets you on your way through life so that you cannot forget or conceal it. If you will let it be really true you will be taught to pray aright. Not before; not one moment earlier!

Pray, why should the new year not begin for you with this, that you will let it be true, I am ill? Praise God, whatever else may be the matter with me, I do not belong to those who are well and therefore not in need of a physician! I am not so rich that I am not finally disturbed about and in myself! I am not so calmly confident of finding another way out of my affliction than the way of calling upon God. See, if you would let it be true today, you may perhaps forget it again tomorrow. But you would surely come back to it again. You would have to let it be true again and again; and thus this New Year would perhaps become a year of new life. For it would be a year with a few open doors and a few possibilities of real prayer.

Our text asks us a second question. The man in Scripture prays. He prays for salvation for himself and for his people. The whole of the eightieth psalm is full of strong crying. His question is this: Would you be whole? It is not at all self-evident that man

would be well. Perhaps we are standing in the open
door of suffering and yet fail to pray for health because
we are not in dead earnest about a change. There is
such a thing as playing with life's misery, both with
one's own or with that of others. And, oftener than we
imagine, we are doing this very thing. There is such a
thing as becoming accustomed to it. We may consider
it necessary, as one needs a companion with whom one
quarrels occasionally but would not really want to miss.
We chafe under our misery; we wrestle with it, but
approve of it after all and always recall it. We have
not been really serious about misery being really misery.
Especially when we have not yet become aware, or have
forgotten again, that behind our misery hides somehow and somewhere also our guilt, we are likely to play
with misery.

Perhaps we have passed from the old into the new
year in such an attitude toward our misery. Then it
is time to consider that at the place where the word of
God would lead us, one does not only groan, but groan
against illness seriously, sorrowfully, full of hostility
and hope. The spirit of Holy Scripture is Holy Spirit,
a spirit of real prayer, because, from the first page to
the last, the Scriptures resound with rebel cries against
life's misery. Deliver us! Deliver us from the evil!
Deliver us from the evil one! On every page is written resentment that things are as they are. It is full of
impatience and yearning. In tones which fill one almost
with alarm God is being importuned at last, at last to

consider and bring to an end the misery of His people.
The Bible tells us that Jesus Christ Himself "groaned
in His spirit" at the grave of Lazarus because of death's
power over man and because forlorn men have only
tears! We are not Jesus Christ. But neither are we
His disciples, and His grace has not yet really found
us, *if* in the gates of suffering we remain standing dumb
or merely wailing.

This is the other question which we are being asked
today: Have you resisted unto blood? If not, dare
we say that we really mean to become whole? Perhaps
the most practical thing that many of us need to be told
in this hour is this, that we are quite differently disposed
than the people whom we hear praying in the Bible.
We do not wrestle with temptation at all. It does not
appal us at all that things are as they are. We have re-
signed ourselves to what we call our fate. If we mean
to pray aright, we need a decided change. The new
year must make a new beginning with us in this respect.
It is true indeed that no one of us knows what true recovery is. We are not the physician, we are the patients.
We cannot in a headstrong manner demand and bring
it about that our misery shall end so or so.

Neither in words, thoughts nor deeds can we make
disposition over the manner in which we shall be delivered from evil. Only in great humility can we rebel
against our illness. But humility which is without hope
and without resentment is not the humility which is
capable of praying. To pray means to have a will to be

saved from the illness which lays us low. If you do not care for recovery—because you do not care for a change in you—how can you be surprised and how can you angrily bewail that matters do not change. Is it not true that real constraint would long since be present to will to be well, to a serious consideration of the enemy without which God is not a serious concern with us.

But again: Why should not the new year make this beginning for you that you really understand this constraint? Why not become honest and reach out for the salvation which is not offered in mockery? Oh, you will often enough have relapses as you loiter about the gates of suffering. But here also it is possible that after you have once taken note of what is really necessary you will in consequence rise again and again in the power of obedience. See, it is possible that this new year could become for you a year of blessing if by God's grace you were compelled, perhaps only once or twice, really to want to be whole. In the power of this obedience you would pray aright once or twice, and this year would be a good year for you, even if it were your last year on earth.

And now let us not be wearied to be asked a third question. It is the most urgent of them, and also the most decisive. The man of Scripture at whose feet we sat down, in the midst of his sorrow and with an urgency of which his words are witness, called upon God. Therefore he prayed for this remarkably simple thing, "Turn us again! Cause Thy face to shine!" He did not ask as a first thing for salvation, and not for salvation as such. In spite of the torture and in spite of his yearning for health and salvation, he asked first that God would turn again him and his people, and cause His face to shine. It means that he called upon God to become again merciful and strong. If this takes place, he knew, salvation will have come. In this he sought it, and it is indeed the third question we are asked, Do you care to affirm this order of things? Do you admit that you must affirm it because you understand that this is the only right way? See, it may well be that we suffer and groan for salvation and still fail to pray aright because we do not yet call upon God.

Perhaps we do not yet comprehend that the misery of our life which we know only too well has its origin in God, because He is far from us; no, because we are far away from Him. The turning point in our misery must come in turn from God, if our misery shall be turned. Perhaps we groan unfruitfully and enter the new year with such unfruitful yearnings because this order of our misery and its change, because God himself has not become vital to us as the One who lays a burden upon us, but also helps us bear it.

It is true after all that our life has a Lord. Because we daily forsake and deny this Lord, our life becomes full of misery and care and becomes a burden and a problem. He is our sickness. His absence is his wrath. Darkness rules where one has withdrawn from His light. In remaining faithful where we are unfaithful, in forgiving sin and showing mercy and patience, in turning us again and causing His face to shine: in short, in remaining our Lord also in the dark places in which we have wandered lies our salvation. In these things we live—a miracle in our eyes!—our daily life. To pray means to seek for this Lord of our life, to search for God who is both merciful and holy. In fact, then, do not seek first salvation, but seek Him first.

Have we comprehended and apprehended this "first"? Everything, yes, everything may depend on our not yet standing where every one who prays aright stands: in the truth, in freedom, in the right order. Perhaps we are altogether too much those who are too well to be in need of a physician, and people who are ill but do not care to become well for the reason that we have not yet comprehended and apprehended this "first." Oh that we could say, We have comprehended and apprehended. We would not need to worry an answer to the two preceding questions. But, who can say this of himself? Who must not confess that he has not yet even begun to comprehend and apprehend? But if we have comprehended and apprehended, then, oh, then it was certainly God's grace and not our work.

Is it not now very, very clear that we can ask only to be taught to pray aright as one asks for grace? He has already been turned, for him His face has already begun to shine who seeks salvation really of Him. No new year's resolution is possible here. Here is possible only fervent prayer and calling upon God, if the

word of God has called us up to do so; and the grace
of God, who will not forsake us in the fervent prayer
and strong crying which He has himself created and
wrought in us; for He is for us with all the power of
salvation in our fervent prayer. Adoration, adoration
alone is possible here: Of Him, and through Him and
to Him are all things. Even my and your poor little
life. To Him be praise unto all eternity!

XII.

"THERE SHALL BE SIGNS"

And there shall be signs in sun and moon and stars; and upon the earth distress of nations, in perplexity for the roaring of the sea and the billows; men fainting for fear, and for expectation of the things which are coming on the world; for the powers of the heavens shall be shaken. And then they shall see the Son of man coming in a cloud with power and great glory. But when these things begin to come to pass, look up, and lift your heads; because your redemption draweth nigh. And then he spake to them a parable: Behold the fig tree, and all the trees: when they now shoot forth, ye see it and know of your own selves that the summer is now nigh. Even so ye also, when ye see these things coming to pass, know ye that the kingdom of God is nigh. Verily I say unto you, This generation shall not pass away, till all things be accomplished. Heaven and earth shall pass away: but my words shall not pass away. But take heed to yourselves, lest haply your hearts be overcharged with surfeiting, and drunkenness, and cares of this life, and that day come on you suddenly as a snare: for so shall it come upon all them that dwell on the face of all the earth. But watch ye at every season, making supplication, that ye may prevail to escape all these things that shall come to pass, and to stand before the Son of man.—*Luke 21:25-36.*

"There shall be signs"—we have just heard, and there follow words telling of these happenings: remarkable pointers toward mighty movements and changes in the heavens and upon the earth, in nature and in history. Sun, moon and stars shall participate, the sea and, not last, mankind too in anxiety and perplexity.

How do we fare in the face of these words? We have listened to them, here in this Church, out of the Bible, yes, even from the lips of Christ Himself. But let us be honest: is it not nevertheless true, that these words merely arouse our curiosity? Their inner content is obvious in the "world" that arouses us in its peculiar way, every morning, as we take our newspaper in hand. It is the "world," more or less calamitous, perhaps dangerous in its stirring natural tumultuousness, which has struck us in various and grievous ways, particularly in this year. And this world of confusion, revolution, and threatening in all of man's relationships, which we have experienced for some time almost daily, has made us fairly hold our breath. What is this world coming to? That makes all of us curious. But, then, we may react a bit, anxious or sympathetic, or sorrowful, or even haughty, as we are "hit" so or so, as these happenings are distant or close to home. The last result of such curiosity is indifference.

But that may not be true. Happenings of the kind related in our text could easily take place this afternoon or at any hour; they could take place even now. Why not? But what then? Undoubtedly there would be a stir; perhaps insanity, furor might grip us. Let us hope that in such an event we might not be lacking in wisdom, action and mutual helpfulness. Profoundly smitten and jarred, we would realize that a terrible storm had broken upon us. But even the most terrible storm comes to an end. And I ask you: What does the great tragedy of Lyons mean to us? The catastrophe of Altdorf? And the destruction of the English dirigible? And the earthquake in southern Italy?

We will not be able to confess ignorance about these questions, for newspapers and tabloids, telegraph and movie, have told us of them. But what of today? Are these happenings any different from the crushing things that are happening closer home? Not two weeks ago the Rhine flowed through our streets. What eventually was this? All of us recollect—to name something really great—the terrors of the war. There are certainly some among us today, who, out of the awful proximity, have seen things with their own eyes, and could tell us things unbearable to hear. But what has that to do with today? There are happenings in every one of our lives which have actually occurred like those related in our text. But what of today? Certainly there is still memory, deeply engraven—but slowly fading memory.

Certainly there are still wounds, perhaps slowly healing wounds, but nevertheless healing wounds. After every one of these events, and were they even the most terrible and incisive, life demands its right, even of those who have been personally affected, not to mention those who are mere spectators. For all this becomes old history, slowly but surely it becomes an old story, in which no longer all, and by and by but a few, interest themselves, because more and more these events are immersed under a multitude of new ones. And some time, perhaps in the dim distant future, the trail of the event shall be obliterated.

So we see that many, if not all, of these happenings indicated in our text might become events either in our vicinity, or in our very midst—but even after we had regarded them with a curiosity that leads to indifference, in the end we would "let things ride" and go our old accustomed way. Man is an adaptable and tough creature and does not allow himself to be upset so easily. Movements and changes in the heavens and upon the earth, in nature and history, are after all only temporal movements and changes, and their consequences for us are always temporary, even when they affect us ever so violently and directly. If Jesus had simply wanted to tell us about specific coming events of this sort He would not have added these words: "My words shall never perish." The content of His words would then have belonged to heaven and earth, of which He Himself said: "They shall perish." Then He would not have spoken—what we usually recognize about His words—eternal words.

But it may be that the reverse is true, that we have not really listened seriously to His words if we listened only because of curiosity; if we heard only references to the *happenings* that are to be. He does *not* say: "*This* and *that* will happen," but He does say, "There shall be signs happening . . " This event and that event

shall be a pointer (indicator). What happenings?
Those events in the happenings of the world, like those
which we have just heard about, of which the newspapers are, and shall be, full; whose eyewitnesses we
are and shall be.

Jesus spoke of no events except those that can take
place before our very eyes in nature and in history as
long as the world has stood and will stand. Yet He
told His disciples that these events would be pointers.
So if we hear only because of curiosity, still we do not
really hear the *meaning* of the words. It makes no
difference to us whether events are past or still to come,
it may refer to none or all of them. The main question
is, "Do we hear that these familiar and all too familiar
events which take place before our eyes are *signs?*"

Signs are important and noticeable things, not because of what they are in themselves, but because of
what they indicate; not what they are in that they
exist, but what they say. "That," says Jesus, "is what
the mighty things in nature and history do as they
eventuate before our eyes. They shall point! They
are to say something. They shall be A B C's, words,
sentences. Who has eyes to see, he shall read, see and
understand."

"They shall clearly and pointedly indicate," says He,
"so clearly and pointedly as the leafing of the trees indicates the coming of spring." In spite of their variety
they shall possess a distinct alphabet. They shall all
point somehow to the characteristic of disintegration,

of "agingness" and of oncoming fatigue, of a "coming-to-an-endness." It is the dirge that vibrates eventually through all the world catastrophes of every sort and of all times, whether out of the dim past or the near present, the sound of the scythe that passes through the grass. "Beware, pretty flowerlet." This is what one finds in the newspapers, but only one who has learned *how* to read. That is the scarlet thread that runs through natural history and the history of the nations. That is the alphabet to which all signs point unitedly: "Heaven and earth shall pass away."

These signs are not *that* to which the signs point, nor that about which these A B C's and words tell, just as the leafing of these trees is not the Spring itself. But these signs and A B C's are only commas, interrogation and exclamation points. One could say they are like the whirlpool and the dashing waters indicative of the nearness of the rapids, such as we have below the rapids of the Rhine.

These indicators are before the eyes of us all. They are clear and distinct. But one must learn to read them. One must know the alphabet in order to read. Otherwise we might not notice these events as signs, but merely as chance natural occurrences and go our way of curiosity and indifference. Or we might confuse their language with another language, as Chinese and Japanese are confused, and thus actually fail to see what is shown to us and not hear what is said to us.

This empirical knowledge *about* these things is evident; to that end we do not need Christ. But the knowledge of the *why* of these things, that they are signs— the knowledge of the *character* of these events and signs, and the knowledge as to what they point to—that is not evident, nor is it to be taken for granted! For this reason we need Christ. And here is where the spirits of men are divided sharply and bitterly, and eventually right here in our midst, in this Church—divided into the knowing and the unknowing, the seeing and the blind, the hearing and the deaf.

Let us take care and not place ourselves too quickly and definitely on either side, neither cautiously to the right nor doubtfully to the left. We cannot place ourselves here nor there, but *we are placed* either here or there. Jesus never took for granted that Peter belonged to the class that understood, for He never felt that He did not *need* to tell him about these signs— nor did Jesus take for granted that Judas belonged to those who did not understand, for He never felt that He did not *desire* to talk to him about these signs. He *had* to talk to Peter and He *desired* to talk repeatedly to Judas. But the fact is that He did this. And the same thing is true of us in this Church—the spirits of men are divided to the end of days. They divide into those who understand and those who do not understand, these who are accepted or those who are rejected, and there is no bridge so carefully or so skilfully built that can bridge from hither to yon.

Let me make this clearer. I could not, in this hour,

even with the utmost love and skill, *prove* to a single one of you that you are foolish to walk the way of curiosity and indifference in the face of these natural and historical happenings; that these events are not merely empirical, but pointers. Whoever sees in this text only tediously long strokes of the pen, with commas—his eyes will have to be opened by Jesus Christ or they never will be opened. Further, taken for granted that we see and understand, of course we would have to deal with letters and words—but then the *character*, the real language and alphabet, would be known, whence it was taken; then we would catch the tone of the scythe which passes through the grass: "Heaven and earth shall pass away." Then I could preach with the tongue of man and angel about the transitoriness of the earth. Then I could make the most pungent statements that ought to be made about these things. I could recall to your minds what are regarded as the surest and most inevitable consequences of all the world tempests which have visited this sphere; those newly dead for whom that sign was a sign, whether they recognized it or not—a sign of the end.

If anyone protests that this is one-sided, exaggerated and profuse pessimism, when we regard this event in nature and the domain of man as relating to this sign that heaven and earth shall pass away, then let his luxurious imagination dwell upon the majesty of death, upon those ten millions who were destroyed in such a short time. One can see the majesty of death, and yet not *see* it. We have to do here not with optimism or pessimism, but with the ultimate reality of our lives.

Jesus can tell us or we shall never know. As if the understanding of this A B C, the understanding of *what* it points to, was just *beginning* to be understood! If it came to reading through this eventful transitory world—so as to see in the passing the coming and the abiding, in the autumn the spring, in disintegration integration, in no yes, in death life, in the dissolution of all earthly kingdoms the imminent approaching Kingdom of God—do you imagine that there is a single philosophy, theology, or art that can teach us to read this wonderful language? Christ will teach us this language, or we shall never learn it.

How could it be otherwise? What might we learn and see here if we could only read and see? Jesus Himself, even He, Who alone can make us seeing and understanding ones as regards these signs; He must speak the word of eternal life so that we can hear: "Heaven and earth shall pass away." These signs are *His* signs, signs of *His* coming and His future.

But you ask me, "Is He not come already? Do we not live in His presence? Do we not have His eternal words? Do we not have the Church, sermon, sacrament, faith and its assurance? Do we not have Christianity, and in it the reality of His grace, life and fullest spiritual abundance? Do we not annually celebrate Christmas as His actual coming, the advent of the great conqueror, Immanuel, God with us?" Yes,

we do; and so we should. Yes, we have Him. And
He is with us. He is with us in the only way He can
be with us, 'twixt heaven and earth, in the very midst
of natural history and the history of mankind, which
are subject to the law of dissolution. He is with us
as the One Who lived in *this* world, Who was born in
poverty and lowly obscurity (concealment), Who died
upon the Cross as a criminal.

Because of the dissolution of this world, His sign
is the sign of death. That means, He is with us
incognito and not in evident ostentatiousness, external
power and glory. He is with us hiddenly, imprisoned
in the dissolution of the world and safely enclosed in
the faith of those who see and understand and possess
Him. He is *nevertheless* with us, in spite of the fact
that everything in this world, as far as the eye can
see, deteriorates, and that in this world we can only
believe what we can never fully see. But this *"nevertheless"* points beyond to a *"therefore"* that will remain for us, in this earthly life, intangible, for which
we must wait and hope, but which we cannot see and
tangibly actualize. We cannot build a physical state
(organized society) upon that *therefore*.

We, as Christians, faithful or unfaithful, will continually be forced to say, to plead, "Abide with us."
We will have to hear afresh and repeatedly His eternal
words in order to possess them. We will never get beyond the experience that our faith is a constant struggle
with our own overwhelming doubt. His revelation as

well as His resurrection will always appear to us as a logical and a physical absurdity. We will regard ourselves as miracles, and if we do not stop at that, even in our best moments, we will regard ourselves as condemned of God. Our rest will be in the midst of unrest, our order will be an order in the midst of disorder. The sermon and the sacrament will by their very nature portray always and distinctly the true character and questionability, and announce the truth, of this transitory world.

The Church and Christianity will always be subject to the law of humility. She will always be an annoying, disagreeable and, in the deepest sense, an unedifying spectacle when she forgets that, and parades herself before the world as an ostensible power—she can and must not desire that. Christ, for us in this world, is the One of Whom it is truly said: "He does not cry nor call, and His voice is not heard in the streets." Who will not profess Him as such, who will not love Him *incognito* and in concealed humility (secret loneliness) will never really possess or love Him. So it will be to the end of time. The glory of His form as a servant can be removed only by Himself, who took it upon Himself for our sake. Thus He came to us. Thus is He with us now.

He shall and He will come to us, however, in an altogether different way, as stated in our text, "in the clouds and with great power and glory." What does that mean? It means that He will not come in secret and concealed fashion, *incognito,* but in open, public preponderance; no, in public sovereignty. So that no one can ignore His righteousness, so that every opposition to Him will be overruled, annihilated and despatched; that the forgiveness by which He has translated us and has forgiven even the least of these brethren may be manifested; that there may be made manifest the sacrificial offering which He has given for our life, the hope which makes the light of our life (which is not a, but *the* only hope), outside of which there is nothing but night and transitoriness. That there may be no escape from His judgment, that there may be only two kinds of people: those who in all eternity shall be adjudged liars and fall victims to death, and those who through all eternity shall be united to the God of all blessedness There will be no *nevertheless* necessary; only a *therefore* will remain.

So then the Church and theology, the sermon and the sacrament, which were necessary forms of His previous *incognito* appearance and presence, shall have reached the finish of functional power and weakness. Then faith shall no longer be needed, for where unbelief is no longer possible, faith will no longer be necessary. Then the promise, yes, the Advent-season will once for all be finished, fulfilled. Then a Christmas season will come which will not be followed by the New Year and Passion season, which now somehow puts our Christmas in a quandary.

Then all the tears which we must repeatedly weep

will be dried, tears which we weep primarily because
He is with us; all thirst and hunger which we suffer,
because we have Him, will be stilled; all burdens will
be lifted, which weigh us down primarily because He
has come into this dissolving world. For just that (His
holy coming into the unholy world) makes us really
sorrowful, hungry, thirsty and encumbered, because
He too seems to be imprisoned and forlorn in this
world, because we find it continually necessary to believe that the best we possibly can have here is after
all only a propping crutch—happy as we are in its
possession—yet we are constantly bitterly reminded of
the fact that we are sick, in the hospital.

There is another *"coming"* of Jesus Christ, His second coming, His second advent, "in the clouds with
great power and glory." It is in the nature of the case
that we cannot imagine this advent, and that we stam-
mer in our attempts to speak of it. How can we be
satisfied with a mere first advent? How shall we
adequately understand the first unless we strain in
every fibre toward the second advent? Should we not
let all our inner and outer peace, security and safety,
which we arduously provide for ourselves and enjoy,
be dissolved and swallowed up in the security and cer-
tainty of this future hope of fulfilment, this revealed
Kingdom of God? Unto this hope alone are we regen-
erated—for what else?

These signs point to this Kingdom. Why? Because
they are all signs of dissolution of the transitory glory

of this present world-kingdom. Whoever has learned
of Jesus Christ, and has had his eyes opened by Him,
will not see primarily the change and decay of this
world, but in its perishing the Cross of Jesus Christ
and that Cross as the promise of His resurrection, and
the resurrection as the promise of His sovereignty—
His coming in the clouds with great power and glory.
Certainly here there is nothing to be taken for granted,
because all things are gifts and grace of God. He who
has been made to see by Christ, he of all men, will discover to his great sorrow the truth of the dissolution
of the world.

Then he will learn what real grief is, in the face of
the sunset glow in which our fair world is bathed, in the
face of the judgment toward which it swiftly reels, in
the face of the great change to which it is subject.
But is not the world that into which Jesus Christ
came? Is there nothing to salvage, nothing to make
secure? Should Christ and we let death be the victor?
Would it not be worth while to cleave to her with par-
asitic tenacity as long as she is not yet dissolved? Yet,
it is remarkable but true, that particularly the disciples
of Jesus had to be told, "Look up and lift your heads."
And again, "Take heed to yourselves in case your hearts
become overpowered by dissipation and drunkenness
and worldly anxieties . . . " We need faith in Jesus
Christ, that both the sorrow and the lust of this transitory world may not become a real temptation.

Who does not have faith has, in this respect, an
easier and more complacent existence. But he who has

faith, he alone has reason to consent to the world, because it is the world, and the stable of Bethlehem is in it, over which the angels sang their Gloria. Yet he hears the call and the warning from beyond. He sees and reads the signs and eventually does not go wrong in that satanic temptation. Not that he has any peculiar gift that was not given to him that did not need to be constantly renewed. But particularly the disciples, particularly the faithful, need to be told, "Pray, that you may succeed in escaping all dangers to come, and may stand before the Son of Man." They are of themselves not able to flee this and stand there of themselves. And it is not *their* praying that accomplishes the task.

They see in their act of believing and praying the very Cross of Christ, the death-conquering Christ of glory, and, as a result, they can never deny their hope though they fall away from Him a thousand times. Because they know Him as the *crucified* One (the helpless *incognito* who now suffers because of the world's power over Him), therefore they are thrown back upon *hope*. They will often desire to run back, they will often be found among the hopeless. But He remains the One He has always been, and will never forsake His own. They will often desire to break away, but they will find the bolt fastened and they can do nothing but *wait* for redemption upon the Son of Man, "coming in the clouds with great power and glory." Praise be to God, that He does not let us fall, and that he remains our immovable God even in the midst of our constant falling.

XIII.

THE NEW BEGINNING

In that hour came the disciples unto Jesus, saying, Who then is the greatest in the kingdom of heaven? And he called to him a little child, and set him in the midst of them, and said, Verily I say unto you, Except ye turn, and become as little children, ye shall in no wise enter into the kingdom of heaven. Whosoever therefore shall humble himself as this little child, the same is the greatest in the kingdom of heaven. And whoso shall receive one such little child in my name receiveth me: but whoso shall cause one of these little ones to stumble, it is profitable for him that a great millstone should be hanged about his neck, and that he should be sunk in the depth of the sea. Woe unto the world because of occasions of stumbling! for it must needs be that the occasions come; but woe to that man through whom the occasion cometh! And if thy hand or thy foot causeth thee to stumble, cut it off, and cast it from thee: it is good for thee to enter into life maimed or halt, rather than having two hands or two feet to be cast into eternal fire. And if thine eye causeth thee to stumble, pluck it out, and cast it from thee: it is good for thee to enter into life with one eye, rather than having two eyes to be cast into the hell of fire.

—*Matthew 18:1-9.*

Jesus places children before us. He uses them as a parable in order to say something decisive to us. Children are people who still stand at the beginning of life. Our questions, those questions of grown-ups and adults, have no meaning for them as yet. And still less our

answers, all these profound, clever and serious phi-
losophies of life which we have constructed for ourselves.   Before children, life lies as yet unspoiled.   For
them everything is filled with possibility and promise;
life is an open book filled with unwritten pages.   With
them so many things are possible.   With us grown-ups
there is much, oh, very much, that is no longer possible.

For us it is too late for almost everything.   We do
not have an undeveloped life before us.   On the contrary, we have run ourselves fast into ruts or run our
lives into an *impasse*.   And when we are asked to consider—and we are asked through this word about becoming as children—where have I run myself fast or
into an *impasse*, it would involve some very painful
and shocking discoveries and confessions.   I would have
to start off with experiences of my own life and you
would have to follow with yours.   For there is not a
single one among us who would not have one or more
spots in his life on which he could put his finger and
say, "Ah, I am no more like a child who can and ought
to begin every day with new hope."

To illustrate with something simple, even though
this condition is difficult enough for us, namely, we have
become fossilized in our vocation, our work.   Day after
day we do it in the office, the factory, the workshop, or
at home in the house.   We do our work without joy.
We begin our work in the morning and, heavily bur-
dened, we return from work at night.   We do what we

have to do, but we work as in a treadmill.   Or, what is worse—I am thinking now of the so-called professions, of us pastors, teachers, doctors, and lawyers—we do our work in routine fashion.   The wheel turns, we earn our salary, but don't ask how!

Externally everything is empty—wheels running, but it is an empty grind, has been for years and years. Another, to mention another, thing which lies deeper: We have married; we live as man with wife, as wife with husband, as parents with their children, as workers with fellow-workers.   But we have gotten into ruts together.   What of the joy, the life, the thrill, the dynamic element that we must have in common, if we are to endure life together?   We are faithful in our married life, but we simply drag it along as though it were a burden.   How many marriages are being dragged along like that!   How great a void is there between parents and children, friends and friends!

Still more important: our faults, our failings, our sins.   Already as children we glided into these sins.   At first we resisted them, but more and more they entwined us like a creeper plant that would hinder us in walking freely.   Today we scarcely resist at all.   But we groan and suffer.   Is not this the really burdensome feature about growing older, that we are forced to see, in so many ways, that going back again is no longer possible?

But listen!   "Unless you turn and become as little children."   What does that mean?   Surely something!

It means—we cannot understand this otherwise—it must mean, "There is, yes, there is a possibility of going back." There is such a thing as a new beginning! There is possibility, hope, future, youth—yes, and for us, precisely for those of us who have become stuck fast, who have run ourselves into a corner, who have grown old, even standing at death's door. Jesus does not try to fool us. When he says "Unless you turn and become as little children . . ." He means "You can, you may; go do it!" That is Jesus, through Whom, for Whose sake, in Whose presence there is this possibility of a new beginning in a life that has already grown old. We have really said everything that can be said about Jesus when we say that. To come to Jesus means to let Him tell us that. It means that to be an old scarred man, in just such a predicament as we have described, one without hope, without possibilities, and then, of a sudden, to face this: "Come to me all ye that labor and are heavy laden, and I will revive you!"

We must not understand that revitalization which comes from Jesus to mean that we must become actual children, childish people. But it indicates that, though we are stuck fast, we may yet come to a point where life begins anew. We did say a moment ago that in many external and internal things we cannot go back again. But in the main thing we can go back. And because it is possible in this main thing, therefore, in a greater measure and degree than we dare think, it is possible in the countless external and internal non-essentials of our lives.

There is a new beginning, and a new creation possible in Jesus Christ, which reaches clear down where we are fettered in body and soul, yes, into sickness, and life's every need. We can! Oh, let us hear, let the Gospel tell us, "We can!" Now, do not interpose immediately and say, "No, I cannot; I am too old; too fossilized; nothing in life can be made new again." Indeed, we can! This is the grace of God in Christ which frees us from the old, hopeless idea, which says: "No use to try; I simply can't." Certainly you can! Rise up and walk. Christ gives you hope and a future. Oh, that we could only hear and see that!

Of course, this does not mean that we can rise up in *our own* strength, and by our own efforts renew our life from within. It is *not* the case that we have within ourselves this new beginning, perhaps covered by a little rubbish, yet, nevertheless, with our own twisting and turning, and by poking (seeking) around within ourselves we can bring the new beginning to the light of day and sort of discover it as a miracle and enter into it. That kind of thing is being shouted at us nowadays from all sides, right in connection with the spiritual situation of today. More than one trickster and magician stands ready who promises to show us the approach to this new beginning which lies hidden under rubbish in us. Beware of such tempters! For this new beginning, to which the words of Jesus refer when He speaks about the children, lies not *in* us, not, as one said, unfortunately, within us. It lies without, beyond.

This new beginning about which Jesus speaks is *God*. Yes, this is God, undoubtedly that God of Jesus Christ, that One, Living, Merciful One, Whose mercy consists in that He has prepared for us such a new beginning of life, such a great redeeming "You can!" From this God this new beginning of life has moved toward us. It is close at hand, it is promised to us, placed before our very eyes as the great, new possibility in the midst of our impossible, old life.

That is the Kingdom of Heaven about which the words of Jesus are so full. That is Jesus Himself; this movement of the Kingdom of God from God toward us, so that from now on we may say "Immanuel, God with us, God among us!" And it is meant thus that we should let ourselves be directed to this God "with all our heart and with all our might," until, as Jesus said, we would rather lose one eye, one foot, than separate ourselves from this God and that which He has prepared for us. Yes, we should be really radical, totally one-sided, as we cleave to and cling to this God and His promise. Yes, this is the new beginning, this determination never to relinquish the gracious and merciful word of this God.

We are thinking of Martin Luther. If I have understood anything of the reformation of the sixteenth century it is this one thing: The fathers of that time again entered into this one-sided, radical "holding fast," not to the possibilities in themselves, but "holding fast" to the word of God which spoke to them from outside of themselves in Jesus Christ.

We could simply say with these fathers, "Forgiveness of sins is what is meant by the passage about becoming as children, although this particular word about sin, as such, is not found here." For, what is sin? Sin means separation from God. Sin may be anything in my life that forces me away from, and shuts me off from, making this beginning; everything which allows me to miss the road or to run into a blind alley. These old walls and partitions are pierced. Jesus broke through them. I can, I may, I am free! That is what He tells me. This is the forgiveness of sins.

Why are we so deaf that we will not be told this? Why will we not be told: You are not the one you pretend to be, as others know you; you are not what you have made of your life, that small, cramped prison you have built up around yourself in your bitterness, and this isolated life of yours, your worries and your sins? You can leave it; it is really only an encasement around you in which you have crept away. Jesus Christ calls you out of it, and because He tells you you are something altogether different from what you are, you are a child of the Father forever.

It may be that we have come more closely to these great things than we were for a long time. This forgiveness of sins as a new beginning of life in God, that

is the thing which in all the gloom of the times is beginning to dawn upon us again, as a light in the darkness
of night.   For today we have driven ourselves into
ruts and must see for ourselves that things cannot go on
this way much longer or we will tumble into an abyss.
In our opinions, our ways and our ideas we have become
altogether so uncertain that we have become, like soil,
loosened to receive the great hope which says: "There
must be a future, and we will go forward."

Finally, we are pointed beyond our human capacities
and possibilities so indubitably that we cannot help but
recognize the fact, "In Jesus Christ, and only in Jesus
Christ, can we go on."   Thus our age faces the portals
of the Kingdom of God.

Having said this, the responsibility resting upon men
in our day is particularly heavy.   Today, if ever, there
is need not only of people who have been stirred but of
men who stand at attention, inwardly free men, open-
minded people, in order that the Kingdom of Heaven
which is before our doors may come in to us.

Let us look at three more points in this word of the
Bible concerning this new attentiveness, this new readiness which is demanded of us today.   First it says,
"Whosoever shall receive one such little child in my
name receiveth me."   That is also speaking in parables.
This child—this is a *symbol* of that new beginning of
life in God.   "Really," says Jesus, "this new life comes
to you from God.   It knocks urgently at the door of
your old life."

As a child beseechingly approaches us, to be received of us, so there are times in our lives and in the life of generations where the new thing which God wishes to say to us comes very close to us. It may come to us through people who, as Jesus says in this text, belong to the small and humble folks who believe in Him and who carry about in their own lives something of this new beginning from God. I again think of Martin Luther, in whose life an entire age saw what is involved in the fresh founding of life in the power of forgiveness. Such people challenge us simply by what they are. Until we too stand before them and think, "I, too, would like to receive something of that which has been given to this plain and humble person. I, too, would like to begin over again as he did. I would like to come to the place where I could have some hope in my misspent life, hope for the sake of my husband, my wife, my children; hope in my work, hope for a little new freedom, with all that I am fettered to my faults and failings."

But now, have a care! Whoever, in such a moment, takes his hand from the plow and looks backward; whoever thinks, "Oh, no; things will not progress; they will go on as before." Whoever thinks, "I do not want to go along upon this new path where one has to hope and believe; I might make myself conspicuous; that's too 'religious' for me; 'forgiveness of sins' sounds like 'Salvation Army stuff'; and eventually I might be asked whether I read the Bible and whether I pray and go to church; I would rather not have anything to do with that."

Whoever thinks and speaks that way slams the door shut, he misses the opportunity; he is not awake and he is not prepared for that which God would do for him. Such moments come upon us quietly and without any commotion. Whoever expects an immediate, mighty surging up of conversion and awakening has certainly not understood what it means when Jesus knocks at our door like a pleading child. But much, in fact everything, depends upon this; namely, that there are people who will take hold of the latch and open the door.

Jesus goes on to speak in these strong words about "offenses," or "occasions of stumbling." Now "offense" means, in this case, distortion, falsification, twisting. In other words, this new beginning from God is a reality. But now there are human beings who get hold of it, take it into their own hands and make something worldly, something arbitrary, something altogether perverse out of it. Holy things are cast before the swine. That which is godly is disfigured beyond recognition; it is abused, made a laughing stock of, so that shame and wrath rise within one over this distortion of what God had begun so good, so new, so dynamic.

I am thinking of the ecclesiastical politicians, of the party leaders, of representatives of all sorts of movements, who misuse the fire of the Gospel to pursue their own selfish ends for the sake of a little power, and to

set their organizations agoing and bring them to a place
of importance, to occupy the chief seats, to proclaim
their party slogans and line up their followers. I am
thinking of those theologians for whom the free forgiveness of sins is too broad and free. They make forgiveness much smaller; they set up conditions and laws,
and take away the comfort of the sinners and the dying
and once more lock the door of Heaven, which the
Saviour opened so wide. Let us hear how Jesus reckons
with these people. Wrath arises within Him, the wrath
that at one time made him cleanse the temple with the
cudgel. "Out," He says, "away with them!" Sink
them in the depths somewhere, these falsifiers and traders, where they can not come up again, that's what one
should do. Oh that something of this wrath might
arise in our Church!

Of course, we would have to turn this wrath against
ourselves first of all, for we ourselves are these falsifiers
of the Gospel, who give offense time and again; these
tacticians and politicians, who take the things which God
puts into our hearts and turn and twist them into something else, yes, crank up a "movement" with them, anything that is humanistic and glitters on the outside. All
this, just so we do not have to be quiet! But that, we
cannot! Just so we do not need to have patience and to
hope! In spite of the fact that everything depends
upon our coming to this patience and waiting for what
God does, and what remains pure and holy only when
it remains *in His hands.*

Finally, this word about the one-eyed, the crippled, the lame and the maimed who enter into the Kingdom. This refers to those who have resisted on behalf of the things of God unto blood. They have sacrificed to prove their devotion. They have given of their very best, of their very life. An eye, a hand, a foot, they have literally thrown away. Again, this is a parable and these things mean all those noble gifts and possibilities that have been bestowed only upon man. Why have they sacrificed this? Because they saw that, precisely with the strong, the good, the powerful thing in me I stand in God's way. Far better to be poor and helpless, with God, than to be strong and possessive of two legs, but without God. That is a remarkable saying.

Do we perhaps have such capacities and possibilities which are to become a temptation for us to go *our own* ways, to pursue our own plans, and which must be sacrificed, must be surrendered, thrown away, when God calls us into His Kingdom? Perhaps our great intellectual cleverness, with which we examine and judge everything without ever asking: "Is this thinking rightly and honestly done before God?" Perhaps our glibness, our brilliant dialectical ability with which we befuddle other people? Or, perhaps, it is simply our so-called moral integrity, our social prestige, our irreproachableness with which we stand in God's way. The hour could come when the Kingdom comes to us and says: "Away with it all!"

Give up your social prestige of which you are so proud

and which makes you so hard; give up your cleverness, your culture which hinders you from being plain and objective; give up your art of defending yourself and your way of banking on your always being in the right! Far better not to have right on your side; far better to give in and say, "I am no better than others." Far better to be a cripple, one-eyed, disease-infected, to have your reputation questioned and be one who thus became accessible to the grace of God in the forgiveness of sins. We all would be healthy, we would go through life on two legs and take hold two-handed.

Before us probably the picture of Him rises now Who spoke these words, the picture of Jesus Christ. He is not only a cripple, lame, one-eyed, but dishonored, condemned, hanged. In His case entering the Kingdom was by way of that cross, by way of that sacrifice which is without parallel. More than likely we will have to understand all this in a deeper and newer sense. Here something must dawn upon us all. We all want to get *around* the cross. But do we not already surmise something of the fact that precisely those who are healthy, those who have two legs, those mighty and powerful on earth are the ones who are leading this world to destruction? Healing and wholeness come to us from an altogether different source; healing will come to us from those who sacrifice and are sacrificed. Everything hinges on this, that this truth will break forth and out among us.

We are all too strong in ourselves to become really

weak before God, so that He can be strong in us in the power of His forgiveness. This is the strength of the humble and small and, as such, the beginning of the life to which Jesus calls us. "Whosoever humbles himself as this little child, he is the greatest in the Kingdom of Heaven." Therefore, "if you do not turn and become as children. . . ."

XIV.

AFTER PENTECOST

And they continued stedfastly in the apostles' teaching and fellowship, in the breaking of bread and the prayers. And fear came
upon every soul: and many wonders and signs were done through the
apostles.—*Acts 2:42-43.*

And they continued stedfastly in the apostles' teaching. The first Christian congregation was born out of
a terrific shattering of souls. We know the mighty
words of the Pentecostal narrative describing the sudden descent upon the apostles of something new, of the
Holy Ghost. "He dealt with them with regal majesty,
in kingly style!" One might compare the action of
the Holy Spirit at Pentecost with the rule of a despot,
before whom all must trembling bow; but this comparison would fail to do justice to the facts.

No, "as storm and fire," says the Bible, He came
down upon them; that is to say, as a Lord, as an incomparable sovereign. He gripped men, and His hand
was upon them as no tyrant's hand ever was upon his
subjects. And now the storm was over. A pause followed. Men came to themselves again. They stood
up, as it were, and looked about and within them. To

be sure, the thunder of the passing tempest still rolled in the distance; there still was, as the Bible tells in our lesson, fear in all souls and many signs and wonders were done through the apostles. But above all it was necessary that they understand what had happened to them. For this they felt, this they knew, this they saw: Something has happened to us and with us; we are no longer the same. They had gone through a flaming fire. They were men struck by lightning, they were broken, bent, new-molded. Their lives had taken an entirely new direction, as a river is turned into a new channel by an earthquake.

But what had happened? Who was this Lord who gripped them so powerfully? What was to become of them in the clutch of His hand? The pause after the storm became a pause for reflection. That is the meaning of the passage, "And they continued stedfastly in the apostles' teaching." These words describe the time of deliberation following Pentecost, in which the significance of Pentecost is made clear; it is a period different from and shorter than the moment of the fiery tongues and the rushing mighty wind. But it is no less necessary and important. What help are the fiery tongues and the storm of the spirit if they are not followed by sound knowledge and clear insight?

I might cite an example from a much later period of the Christian church. One may compare the awakening of the Bible in the soul of Martin Luther with the events of Pentecost. The mighty Calvin had to

follow Martin Luther and put into fixed forms of doctrine suitable for instruction and as an assurance against
loss in the future what had broken out in Luther as a
flame of fire. What would have become of the Reformation without the profound thinking and the clear
expositions which are preserved for us in the writings
of Calvin?

"And they continued stedfastly in the apostles'
teaching." Yes, into what kind of school and under
what kind of instruction had they now been taken?
What had shaken them and moved them so mightily
that their minds and hearts could not come to rest, that
they must stedfastly ask and seek, begin their lives
anew, once again sit on school benches like first-graders,
who know nothing at all and yet are grown men and
women? I will try to give an answer: They have
changed from men who looked only at their lives to
men who really live their lives because they know their
condition.

Let me make clear by example what I mean. I once
read a story of a man who was hypnotized by a criminal
doctor and in that dreamy state committed murder. He
awoke immediately after, was led to the place where
the deed was done, and was told that he was the murderer. He did not understand it at all and thought
that someone was playing the fool with him. What
he himself had done seemed so distant, so strange to
him; he felt as if he were only a spectator. He was

shocked at the murder; but that it had anything at all to do with him he could not understand. But when they were able to convince him beyond a doubt that the deed was his, then he broke down completely. Then he ceased to be merely a spectator. Then he knew that he and the transgressor were one and the same and that he was undone.

Then no matter how much else of the good and beautiful may be in his life, this deed shows who he really is, it passed judgment on his life; and it seemed to him as if the ground reeled beneath his feet. The awakening of the early Christians through the sermon of Peter on Pentecost was not less significant, not less stormy and weighty. They, too, had lived until now as in a dream. They had looked upon their life as if in reality it did not concern them very much, as if they might in an easy way escape responsibility for it. They were honest and upright, even pious and religious, people. Otherwise they would not have been present to hear Peter's sermon. Of course they had their faults; heavens, who does not have his faults!

If anyone had come to them and said, "Your entire life runs in a false channel! There is nothing, absolutely nothing, good in it, as little as a single step which one takes in the wrong direction can be right; you are staggering toward an abyss," they, like the murderer, would have looked astonished at such an one and thought that he was making sport of them. And yet it was true; not, indeed, before men, but before God! God, the Supreme Judge, constantly looks into the lives of men; and who can stand before Him!

Before men, also before ourselves, we can readily pass muster with the usual explanations and justifications of our lives. We all have laid up a smaller or larger assortment of such explanatory and defensive notions which enable us to come to terms with ourselves. We call it having a world-view (*Weltanschauung*), and we may compare these world-views with a pair of spectacles through which we look at life, our own and others'. Every man has such spectacles. And these spectacles are so adjusted that through them one sees life not as it really is, but as one would like to see it; in other words, sees it idealized.

Now, life is really so constituted that from time to time we begin to observe that, at bottom, it is entirely different from what we wish to see. But we know how to remedy that. In such a case we simply change our spectacles; we accept a new world-view, we seek a new leader, we attach ourselves to a new movement, we read the book of some new spectacle-seller, and so remain dreamers and prisoners. But now and then the miracle may happen: we are shocked so hard that our world-view is shattered; and then we really have to open our eyes and see, and suddenly or slowly we come out of our dream and find out who we really are. We are guilty! Our whole life is depraved through and through. Or, as Martin Luther put it, when he awoke:

"All our deeds, even in the best lives, count for nothing." Is that put too strongly, is it saying too much;
or is it the truth? He who has awakened knows that
it is the truth!

But what was the effect of this discovery upon the
early Christians? A single word explains all: Jesus
Christ! They saw Jesus Christ and saw Him crucified.
They had seen and understood—that was their Pentecost—what it meant that He hung on the cross on Gol-
gotha. Peter through his sermon made it clear to
them that He hung there not by chance. He concerns
thee! As if a curtain had been lifted before their eyes,
they saw the powerful and ever-present indictment that
was there brought against mankind. "He died for my
sins; my depraved life is there exposed, my deep, all
too deep, contradiction to God is there brought to judgment."

They saw themselves for once, and knew who they
were, and knew that there is no escape! Yes, hitherto
they had been spectators of their own sin and guilt.
But now the cross had come toward them as from a
far, far distance. It had come very close to them,
closer than anything else in the world. It came, as it
were, down from the stage right into the audience.
They saw that with this thing they were completely involved. And as a cloud rises suddenly and grows larger
and larger, so grew their sin from a mere speck in a
corner of their lives to a million times its size, so large
that it could not be measured, and hid the heavens from

them. But that is only one thing; they saw also at this time of judgment unexpected grace.

To refer to the illustration in which mention is made of the debt of millions which we can never pay, that we may see what must be made clear through these words, "Then the Lord had pity on his servant and let him go and forgave him all his debt," Lo! that too came toward them as from a far, far distance, and came near, very, very near to them, nearer than any other word in the world, and addressed them as if it had been spoken for them and for them alone. And they understood that He who hangs on the cross and bears our sins bears them in order to take them away—to make them null and void.

They saw, also, that they were sinners, but that they, the transgressors, were washed clean and were forgiven! It was as if a mighty hand appears and with one move brushes away the cloudy darkness of the heavens and with one stroke lights the sun again, brilliant as on the first day. Yes, of forgiveness, too, they had been until now mere spectators; they had known about it, as one knows about such things when one goes to church once in a while on Sundays. "God is gracious!" "God forgives!" Who does not know that! But all too often that does not concern one. Now they really knew what is meant by the words "God forgives!" For now they knew: He forgives me! I am sinful, but my sin is covered!

Behold, that was Pentecost. That was the thunder

and lightning of the Holy Spirit! That was powerfully brought home to the early Christians by the teaching of the apostles. This they pondered, worked out, reflected upon, inquired into, and came to understand. We scent in the word "teaching" something dry, something dusty. But that only shows that we have not been brought to the true doctrine. This teaching appears dusty, dry, monotonous, only as long as we ourselves are mere spectators.

In fact, what do Christ and His cross signify to us as long as we do not know what need we have of Him? He who fancies himself on the right road needs no guide. He who still seeks to help himself will never ask forgiveness. We call ourselves Christians, but we are just as near to, or as far from, the real, first Christians as the teaching of the apostles is near or far from us.

They remained stedfast in the apostles' teaching. But something is added: "And in the fellowship, in the breaking of bread and in the prayers." All this belongs to, makes clear, and gives depth to, what has already been said.

They remained "in the fellowship." That is, they understood themselves. Already, at Pentecost, the great miracle was that a word came and was heard which all understood, and by which all understood themselves. And it was not merely a passing delirium. They continued in it. For they understood themselves to the depths. What were these depths? Once again:

It was this, that they all knew themselves to be sinners, so that none could cast reproach upon the other. That was their fellowship. That is to this day the fellowship of the congregation of Jesus Christ: a fellowship of sinners who live by grace.

This fellowship is the direct opposite of all other fellowships in the world. All other fellowships are founded upon the presumption that men associate upon a common basis of something that is high, good, ideal. But, consider a moment, does that really bring us together? Has not each one another good which he seeks, another ideal that he pursues, another Fatherland that he loves, another family to which he belongs, another mental and moral tendency which seems to him the true one? And is the world full of fellowships? No, full of strife about fatherlands, ideals, intellectual tendencies, of churches and groups and parties with all their ideals and goals.

But how shall we obtain peace? Can we get it otherwise than by coming down from the heights and standing beside each other, that in the depths we shall find ourselves to be brothers and sisters, and none can upbraid the other? We must place ourselves where the first Christians stood; there, where we actually stand already: beneath the cross of Christ, where man becomes a sinner. For the cross of Christ is here, and we also stand beneath it. We are all sinners together. We need only awake in order to realize it. We also, like the first Christians, must enter into the teaching of the apostles in order to find true fellowship, not imaginary, not artificial, but real fellowship with real men.

"And in the breaking of bread": To sinners the bread will be broken. In the depths we reach the true heights. There, where we see that we have reached the end, everything transforms itself into the great beginning; judgment turns into grace. My friends, I speak of the Lord's Supper; not of ours, but of the Lord's Supper of the first Christians. When the great upheaval comes upon men they know again that they are sinners! Then, too, they will also know what is meant by the words spoken to sinners: "Take, eat, this is my body, which is broken for you! Drink ye all of it: this is my blood, the blood of the new testament which is shed for you to the remission of sins!" Then, hungry and thirsty, they reach out their hands for the bread and wine.

We know all this only from afar. The Lord's Supper—ah, it has long since become for us more or less a pious custom. We are not real guests at the Lord's table, but only spectators who attend a transaction which does not concern ourselves. But nowhere ought this to be less possible than here! Again I shall remind you of the Reformation. At that time men were really not much more than spectators of this sacred act.

Behind the screen which shut off the chancel from the nave of the church, the priest celebrated high mass, lifted the chalice and the host and showed them from afar to the believers. That very thing the Reformers refused to endure any longer. They broke through the screen and by force brought down the bread and chalice among the people that they might be fed and their thirst be quenched. They had to do it. For they hungered for actual assurance of forgiveness that was not merely something to look at, but something that really brought them help in their sin and misery. My friends, let us be honest and frank. Would very much be taken from us if the Lord's Supper should once again vanish behind the screen whence the Reformers brought it forth? By this question we may prove to ourselves how near we are to, or how far we are from, the first Christians.

"And in prayer." In this phrase all that has been said is summed up. If we can no longer merely look upon God; if we know that He wants something with us, that He comes toward us in Christ and deals with us after His unfathomable and majestic mercy, then we cannot be silent. Then we also must speak. Then all mere contemplation ceases because He speaks; and through His word our tongues are loosened.

We come to prayer. His speaking to us and our speaking to Him prove that we do not have God merely in our imagination or in our contemplation, but that we know the living God. That is so obvious that it needs no further explanation. The fellowship of transgressors who are saved by grace, the fellowship of sinners and of children, is a praying fellowship.

But where do we stand? Is it not true that this picture of the first Christians, when we put ourselves into it, lures us like a dream? But we are the dreamers. And our dream consists in this, that we think we can really get along without the teaching of the apostles, without continuing in this fellowship of children and sinners, without the breaking of bread and prayer.

This picture of the first congregation breaks into our illusion and dream and it may awaken us. We are not to weave it again into our own dreams. We should not deceive ourselves by entering a new rôle, the rôle of early Christians, which we certainly are not. The danger consists in this. Much is said today of the reawakening of the first love, of living congregations that ought to be founded. Let us beware! Here we have to do with something quite different from the realization of a so-called ideal! The first Christians were anything but an ideal congregation. They were sleepers aroused by fright, men who were shaken. They brought to a finish all sorts of matters, which we shall not do so quickly after them. In their circle they were done with Mammon and with sickness and with the powers of death.

Next Sunday we shall speak of that. But they could do this only through this upheaval, this great awakening. They actually began at the beginning. They differed from us because they would not claim to be farther than they were. That was their awakening. Where were they? With Jesus Christ. There is the beginning. This beginning must also be our beginning. God will let us go on wandering and stumbling about in our dreams as long as we do not begin there. And the mission of the first Christians is to tell us across the centuries that this beginning is also possible to us: Jesus Christ, the same yesterday, today, and forever.

XV.

THE LABORERS IN THE VINEYARD

Then answered Peter and said unto him, Lo, we have left all, and followed thee; what then shall we have? And Jesus said unto them, Verily I say unto you, that ye who have followed me, in the regeneration when the Son of man shall sit on the throne of his glory, ye also shall sit upon twelve thrones, judging the twelve tribes of Israel. And every one that hath left houses, or brethren, or sisters, or father, or mother, or children, or lands, for my name's sake, shall receive a hundred-fold, and shall inherit eternal life. But many shall be last that are first; and first that are last. For the kingdom of heaven is like unto a man that was a householder, who went out early in the morning to hire laborers into his vineyard. And when he had agreed with the laborers for a shilling a day, he sent them into his vineyard. And he went out about the third hour, and saw others standing in the marketplace idle; and to them he said, Go ye also into the vineyard, and whatsoever is right I will give you. And they went their way. Again he went out about the sixth and the ninth hour, and did likewise. And about the eleventh hour he went out, and found others standing; and he saith unto them, Why stand ye here all the day idle? They say unto him, Because no man hath hired us. He saith unto them, Go ye also into the vineyard. And when even was come, the lord of the vineyard saith unto his steward, Call the laborers, and pay them their hire, beginning from the last unto the first. And when they came that were hired about the eleventh hour, they received every man a shilling. And when the first came, they supposed that they would receive more; and they likewise received every man a shilling. And when they received it, they murmured against the householder, saying, These last have spent but one hour, and thou hast made them equal unto us, who have borne the burden of the day and the scorching heat. But he answered and said to one of them, Friend, I do thee no wrong: didst thou not agree with me for a shilling? Take up that which is thine, and go thy way; it is my will to give unto this last, even as unto thee. Is it not lawful for me to do what I will with mine own? or is thine eye evil, because I am good? So the last shall be first, and the first last.—*Matthew 19:27—20:16.*

If we mean, God willing, to hear and to grasp something of what this gospel has to say to us in this hour, it seems to me we must have due regard for the point of view which is required of those who desire to hear the word. Throughout this gospel, faith is spoken of as the obedience of man; as a deed, an action, a performance; as a part of man's living, volition, and achievement, which becomes a fact at a definite time and place. We can and must say with confidence: Faith is spoken of as a work of man. The disciples of Jesus said: "We have left all and followed thee." If the behavior of the disciples is faith, then, indeed, faith is a work. Here are the laborers who first stood idle in the marketplace, then were hired to work in the vineyard; some worked longer and harder than others, but all worked.

Again, if faith is labor in the vineyard, then faith is a work. It is emphatically and disturbingly impressed upon us that the personal, all too personal, issue of the content of this work remains an open question. Only one thing becomes almost terrifyingly clear: this work has to do with this—with everything! with giving up houses, brothers, sisters, father, mother, children, lands. But perhaps this is only the reverse side—the shadow of the work itself, the substance of which we shall find to consist in this: following Jesus, obeying the call of the householder to go into his vineyard and to labor until evening comes.

Our question, "What shall we do?" is not withdrawn, but is to be answered by another question: "Who art thou?" How can you presume to have faith, when you do not know that in faith you have the Lord Jesus as your Master, who has told you long ago and this very moment tells you clearly what really is the work of your faith? For this is the work of faith, not that it is any sort of work that a man thinks he ought to do or to be told by others to do, but that it is the work of direct personal obedience to Jesus as Lord, the following of Jesus at the call of Jesus. Therefore it is attended by that shadow, "We have left all." That is to say, we have no Lord but this Lord; in other words, faith is an act without reservation or conditions. Our gospel sets this faith before our eyes. It asks us, who think we believe, whether our faith is this *work*, whether it is *this* work. It asks us whether our faith may be merely the work of an emotion or of a thought, a very lively emotion, a very profound thought, perhaps, but still such a feeling or thought as plays no part in our actual living. Our gospel asks us, "What have you to do with Jesus?"

Jesus is the Lord who has called you, whom you follow, in whose vineyard you labor; or He is not your Jesus. The faith that is obedience demands *you*, not merely your emotions and your thoughts, however upright and true both may be. It knows naught but itself; no other Lord, either open or secret. Our gospel questions us then, and perhaps just then, when our faith is the work of a very devoted, an outwardly very active, perhaps a very earnest, a very energetic, a very loving, that is to say, a very "Christian," life. "What have you to do with Jesus?" Has He really called you to your seriousness, to your goodness, to your activity, to your decided Christianity? There are other vineyards which belong to other lords.

If, perchance, you serve a wholly different lord, how can you then assume to do My work, the work of faith? Let it be understood: even if one were among us who could really say with Peter, "I have left all—houses, brothers, sisters, father, mother, children lands;" yes, even if there were one among us who at this moment would arise and give his goods to the poor and his body to be burned, our gospel would ask him none the less whether he was really doing the work of faith, the work of obedience. Not that we leave all, but that we leave all in *His name*; not that we go into a vineyard but that we go into a vineyard of the Lord, that is the work of faith.

There is much heroism and self-sacrifice in the world. Well to him and honor to him who is capable of it. But this "Well to him!" and "Honor to him!"

are entirely distinct from the "Blessed are ye!" of the gospels. Let us not forget that even the Devil has his martyrs. It may be that our determination and our strength to work leave nothing to be desired, yet in the light of our gospel we are still like those standing idle in the market place, because we have not thought at all of doing what Jesus commanded us. This, then, is the place in which our gospel puts us, the place in which we must stand in order to be able to hear what it has to say to us.

It speaks further of the reward of this work and of our claim to this reward; which, however, we should on no account plead in our behalf. But all this is said to those whose faith is work, and just this work of obedience to the Lord. We may well ask whether we are such persons, or whether by this presupposition of our gospel we are not already shut out from a deeper understanding of it and would not do better to break off, or to think further on this presupposition. Luther more than once said of our text: It is not "for young folk"; one might translate, not for a chapel service in a university. Why not? Because one may well ask if "the young folk" would not do better to ponder the question of obedience instead of splitting their heads over the question of the reward of obedience and their claim to it.

Just the same, Luther did preach occasionally on this text. And one would have to say that in this respect we are all "young folk," that in this respect the apostle

Peter himself perhaps belonged to the "young folk," to whom the question of obedience must be put again and again. But for all that, there is for them as well as for their elders the grace of God by which this question may be so answered that the "young folk" would be old enough not to be allowed to hear but to have to hear, and then perhaps be able to hear what more our gospel has to say.

Our gospel speaks, as unequivocally as possible, of a reward of faith. The Old and the New Testaments speak of it also in other passages. In the evangelical church this has often been disputed or reluctantly admitted. Men have thought they could describe pure faith by disregarding any attainable aim and thus leave it up in the air. But in this respect men wanted to be more Christlike than Christ, and no longer had the Scriptures on their side.

Even in the sermons of Luther there is at this point too much evasion of that which is written and will be spoken. For here it stands, that Jesus did not rebuke Peter's mercenary and eudemonistic question, "What then shall we have?" but answered it with a description, by no means short, of the reward which obedience brings. And it is written that the householder agreed with the laborers for a penny, and that each one duly received his penny. He who does not like this may say so, but he can say it only in defiance of the gospel. The work of faith, as it is held up to us by the gospel, has a hope, for it has a promise; it has also a reward. And the reward when it is given is not the work of faith itself, as has been beautifully, much too beautifully, said; but it is realized in the assured and joyous expectation of the reward.

Let us speak more precisely: it comes about for the reward's sake. That is not a Catholic but a Christian doctrine. Here it is told us and we must let it be told us. Perhaps many, the older they grow, have concluded that they have reason to be glad when they have let this be told them. The way of faith—one knows it better the longer one tries in the least way to understand it—is a hard, rough road.

If it is true that it always entails leaving everything, then it is a daily impoverishment—in the final analysis a daily dying. And now suppose it were not the Lord, not this Lord, the Lord Jesus, who placed us on this road; suppose it were not a real road, that is, it had no goal!   For the sake of this goal—assuredly for the sake of the Lord, even for the Lord's sake who set before us this "mark of our calling"—the work of faith, of obedience to this Lord, occurs.

It occurs not because He says to us that He desires to have it from us, but because He says that what He will have from us is for our good; because His command has the nature and power of a promise. Just because, according to the Scriptures, faith is never without hope, one can say that already in faith itself we may taste and see how good the Lord is. It were enough if we were only told that the work of faith is done in hope, in expectation of a reward, as a labor which will receive its penny, as a way to a goal.

Our gospel gives us also a description of the nature of this goal. It is decidedly important for the understanding of the whole gospel that we now listen to this description. Jesus told His disciples that they would, "in the rebirth," in the eternal deliverance of the coming kingdom of God, "sit upon twelve thrones and judge the twelve tribes of Israel." And what they now forsake in His name they shall then receive many fold.

This is not a description of a common paradise with every possible and capricious pleasure, such as Mohammed promised the faithful. What Jesus here promises belongs to the substance of the obedience of faith itself—first of all to the obedience of faith of His disciples. Even that which they now do in secret, tried from without and within, in the darkness of a destitute faith, that is, in the darkness of the world and their own worldliness, even that shall be revealed in the regeneration, in the reflection of the unveiled glory of Jesus Himself. And this revelation shall consist in this, that they, the poor fishermen, publicans, and sinners, shall stand judging the twelve tribes of Israel, in the very place where now and only now the so-called great in world history, the supposed but only supposed leaders and heroes of mankind, stand.

What they now lose and must lose, on account of their faith, shall be returned to them not diminished but increased many fold. That will be their penny, that will be their reward. They will become that for which through their faith they are designed to be. We dare go further: Even this we also will become, if our faith is obedient and the Lord is the object of our faith. We shall not be the same as the apostles, but (and this is not something less but something else) that which we in our faith in the Lord, if it is our faith, are intended to be.

We are going, then, not to a fantastic Paradise, not to an eternal hallelujah-singing, but toward a revelation of the distinctive quality of our life as believers, the unique element which is indeed now manifest to the forgiving and healing mercy of God; for to our eyes, and to the eyes of all men and angels, the manifestation of the structure which must consummate the enduring foundation of our faith is still hidden. This is the goal, the reward, the penny, that in us and in all creatures we shall see what is now veiled in faith and can be believed only as an inaccessible and incomprehensible message; that we also shall sit upon thrones or upon footstools—upon which it will then matter little—and shall become what is now assured us only through the promise of the forgiveness of our sins.

Will this essential thing, toward which faith moves, become once again a work, an entirely new and different work, which will attach itself to the obedience in which faith now consists as a second and a later work? One might almost think so when one reads that to the apostles in the regeneration a kind of continuation of

their office will be given. Or shall we understand it
even better if we say that it will not be another, a second work, but our present work on earth, in its essence
seen clearly by God now, but for us wholly in the
future?

We do not know what we say when we repeat from
the Scripture the two words, "eternal life." But perhaps these two words lead in this new direction. But
we have said enough—perhaps too much! He that hath
ears to hear hath heard; not by what has been said but
by what is written. This is sure: the reward will be the
reward of faith; the goal to which the way leads will
be the crown of the work. We are not told this of any
other work, however good. But it is told us of the work
of faith. One is assured again and again that faith shall
be joy. If one were to speak of one's present state as
faith, it would be a phrase that one would not expect
of men. For one's present state as faith is sorrow and
strife, is the burden and the heat of the day, all the
more so the more it is actually faith. But it is joy even
in the present state, for it is hope— "The hope of the
righteous shall be gladness." (Prov. 10, 28).

We should be more humble, and more prudent too,
if we were not ashamed of this promised penny but
would honestly console ourselves in view of it. He
would not be the Lord if He did not give us this comfort. And little does he know his Lord and surely he
labors not in His vineyard who thinks himself too exalted for this penny.

But now, if we want to hear everything, we must, without taking offense, permit ourselves to be led in an entirely different direction. Twice we have heard in our text the warning that the first shall be last and the last shall be first; and between the two stands the parable of the laborers in the vineyard, the story of the exceptional employer who startled the laborers who had served him all day by giving not only to them but to those who came much later, even to those who came at the close of the day, precisely the same wages; of the protest of the earlier and more industrious workers, and of the master's declaration that he is within his own rights and has done them no wrong if he chooses to give to the last even as unto the first. The words about the first and last, at the beginning and the end of this parable, must mean: The first shall be like the last, and the last like the first; the first and the last shall be equal.

There is a place in the New Testament (Luke 13:30) where this word has another meaning. Here certainly it means that the reward of faith is alike for all who really do the work of faith. The thrones of the apostles signify a different, a distinctive, but not a better nor a richer reward. That is their penny, but not more than a penny. The goodness of the Lord is to all who labor for Him, to each in his own fashion—but adapted to each.

Even the parable which follows clearly forbids us to understand otherwise the answer of Jesus about the

wages. But more than that, the parable tells us something singular besides—one might well say, something
disturbing—but at the same time also something necessary and salutary. It reminds us of the fact that those
who engaged in the work of faith and, as we have
shown, have a claim on the reward, such as Peter and
his companions and all of us (even when we are at our
best, namely, in the way of faith) are men not only weak
but wicked, depraved men who badly understand their
Lord in relation to them and therefore also their faith
and their reward; who act in such wise that one must
say they have lost Him and can do nothing better than
turn about and, if they are able, make a new beginning
in faith and obedience.

This wickedness, even of believers, is deeply
impressed upon us by the parable of the protesting
laborers. The protest of the laborers is quite comprehensible, just as comprehensible as the conduct of the
householder is incomprehensible. But surely this comprehensible protest would be incomprehensible, and this
incomprehensible conduct comprehensible, if we rightly
understood the Lord and the faith and the reward, and
if we went about it in the right way. This would come
about if we would take seriously what we know: that
the Lord is the Lord.

Thus our work, the work of faith, our labor in the
vineyard, is to be understood as a permission, as a gift,
as His work, for which we must now and forever be

thankful; thankful, too, for the reward which He has made possible for us by calling us to work for Him.

Such gratitude would not be possible in any human contract to labor, not even in these times of unemployment, when one has come to learn the least bit better that work is a blessing. Only in the contract between God and the believer is such gratitude at all possible. Yet herein faith consists, that one allows the Lord to be the Lord, and ascribes to Him all honor and to His will all righteousness; and, further, that one believes not in his work, not in his faith, but in the Lord from whose hand the work and the reward, the reward and the work, come. And is it not true now that in this freedom which we should ascribe to the Lord, our faith, even when we have it, becomes again and again an open shame? The parable tells us how that comes to light— comes only to light—in the comparison of our faith with that of others.

Should they actually receive the same reward as ourselves? Should the Lord really be so gracious? Yes, why not? If we ourselves abide in faith and ascribe to the Lord all honor and all righteousness, could this question arise at all? Would we not then be much more amazed, even if we were the greatest heroes of faith, not that others, but that we ourselves really receive the reward? Would we then not consider our most modest and questionable brothers and sisters more worthy of this reward than ourselves? Would we not ten times more easily discover this work with reward in the first and best of our fellow sinners in whom we can discern only a stray spark of faith? Would not the goodness of the Lord be much more readily understood by us when it is shown to everyone else than when it is shown to ourselves?

In faith we should have to look away from ourselves to the invisible Lord, to Whom alone the glory of the work belongs; and since we must look somewhere, let us look toward our brethren whom we know and in whom we find a far greater reason for remembering the reward. We should then of ourselves be grouped with them and could rejoice only in this, that we received the same reward as they, the reward for which we could only be thankful.

You know how we stumble at this point. No, we are those who have borne the labor and the heat of the day, who have done the great serious work of faith while the others took it easy because they knew how to spare themselves, and yet were happy, so happy that one may well ask whether they are not half idlers, half or even wholly unbelievers, beside me, the earnest, faithful, weary hard-laborer of the Lord . . . ! Should not God know this? Should not He take account of it? Should not He make a distinction? Should not the greater work give me superior worth and therefore higher wages? Should God be God if this is not so?— Yes: Should God . . . ?— Whence comes the beginning of this argument? Where have we come to now? We shall not follow the matter further. We know it all too well. What becomes evident in it? It is manifest that we have left our task again, the task which is done by faith and in which we thought ourselves to be engaged, and that again we are without a lord.

We must now be glad that perhaps when the Master calls us again we may be not indeed among those who have labored most, but among those who have labored least, only since the eleventh hour; and if we may do penance like the thief on the cross—really no less sincere penance than his—then truly we have cause to rejoice in the ordinance of heaven which each moment in our lordless state we would have overthrown.

That there is such an eleventh hour, even for us believers who, again and again at the height of our faith, must discover ourselves to be unbelievers; that God truly treats us not with wrath but with His incomprehensible goodness, that is the comfort of which we have need so that we may actually comfort ourselves with the comfort of the Promise.

XVI.

THE FORGIVENESS OF SINS

And he entered into a boat, and crossed over, and came into his own city. And behold, they brought to him a man sick of the palsy, lying on a bed: and Jesus seeing their faith said unto the sick of the palsy, Son, be of good cheer; thy sins are forgiven. And behold, certain of the scribes said within themselves, This man blasphemeth. And Jesus knowing their thoughts said, Wherefore think ye evil in your hearts? For which is easier to say, Thy sins are forgiven; or to say, Arise, and walk? But that ye may know that the Son of man hath authority on earth to forgive sins (then saith he to the sick of the palsy), Arise, and take up thy bed, and go unto thy house. And he arose, and departed to his house. But when the multitudes saw it, they were afraid, and glorified God, who had given such authority unto men.—*Matthew 9:1-8.*

These words of Jesus to the sick man are the center of this story. That they could be spoken, and not only spoken but heard and believed by this man, is the primary concern of the narrative. For healing and help followed this assurance of Jesus. Unless these words of forgiveness had been spoken, the disease could not have been cured. Indeed this seems to us to be something quite insignificant. And so it was. Let us consider what really happened.

Here lies a man palsied, in dire need, marked by

fate; and Jesus says nothing else to him than that his sins, the paralyzed fellow's sins, are forgiven. That is all that happened. When we consider this transaction it is hard for us to see in it anything of great moment. It is clear, however, that from the viewpoint of the Bible the greatness of this incident is in its littleness. For the apostles who witnessed this event and who frequently recounted it; for the first Christians who never tired of hearing the story, the breath-taking part of it was the assurance: "Thy sins are forgiven."

These words, going forth from Jesus, as a ray of light piercing the darkness, to the poor creature lying before him were the supreme event, far weightier than all the alarming and tumultous deeds which were then aplenty in the world at large. That this was possible upon earth among men, as is distinctly said at the end of this passage, meant that for the apostles and the first Christians an incomparable moment had come—a moment around which the centuries stand in silence, the moment for which, we are told, not only men upon earth glorified God, but for which the invisible world of the blessed, of those who had finished their course, of spirits and angels, broke forth in joy.

Forgiveness of sins granted unto men upon earth; this is the central fact not only of this story but of all the stories in the Bible. This is the event which the congregation of Jesus Christ is permitted to claim and to proclaim in all the centuries of history. This mystery of forgiveness is for the church the marvelous central message; and one may say that the most magnificent cathedrals and domes of the Middle Ages are not grand enough to enshrine it. Do we, also, sense something of the infinite greatness of what is here announced as fact, though we cannot understand it? For if sins are forgiven on earth, and that means if our sins are forgiven; if we, you and I, perchance now in this hour, here in this church, can be convinced that the word of forgiveness is spoken to me, that my sins are forgiven, then we shall really have been in church, and then the greatest things that can come to us in life will have come to us: help and salvation will have come to us.

Let us see what happened when this event occurred. One can hardly put into appropriate simple phrase the things at issue. Simple indeed what happened: Jesus told a person, who was lying in misery and distress before him, that he was a sinner. That is about all that took place. But we must take heed how Jesus spoke to this man. The man did not first confess to Jesus. Nor is there anything here to indicate that Jesus in an indirect way looked into his life and there found many things that cannot be condoned; but Jesus saw this man lying there, saw his need and his misery, and then uttered as the first word, saying: "You, your sins!" One might almost say that Jesus dealt with this man in a domineering manner.

This address reminds one of the procedure of an arrest where one comes, lays his hand on a man, and leads him away. Thus Jesus lays his hand on this man, and immediately judgment is pronounced: *Sins*. Upon second thought, the manner of the address appears rather severe. We can hardly conceive that this should be the first word directed to this wretched man, even though we remember what must not be forgotten, that the words, *sin, sinner,* are to be quickly submersed in the wholly different word: *Forgiveness* of sins.

Even when we take this into consideration, we might ask: "Why does Jesus here speak thus to this man?" After all, this man lies here before him, came to him in incomparable distress, in misery which is all the more evident because he is helpless on a bed. Yes, he is a palsied man. He who once in his life has seen a paralytic, has seen him without the use of his limbs, which God created for use, has seen how his whole body becomes a fearful prison in which his soul is confined—he who has looked into this prison, this captivity, this shackling of the man with the misery of disease, he knows the wretchedness that lay before Jesus. And He, instead of lending a helping hand, as we might expect (for this is what we did expect), forgives sins.

Why did Jesus proceed in this way; why did he not first say "Arise and walk"? Why did he first say "Your sins, your sins are forgiven"? Yes, why? This question arises when we ponder the story. It should arise, and we want to meet it squarely and not to evade it. Why does Jesus ask about the sins instead of the disease?

There can be no doubt that Jesus really saw the misery caused by the disease of this man. He would not have been who He is if He had not seen it—the distress of body, the need of sympathy, these tormented, crippled, and shackled limbs of this wretched bundle of humanity which they laid before Him. Indeed He sees all this. We must not presume that we are more merciful than He and imagine that we see the wretchedness of this man more clearly than He. He saw it all. He sees it today also. He sees the distress of the crisis in which mankind is today. He sees the hunger of the unemployed, the despair of the masses, who, almost crushed by the crisis, see no way of escape. He sees the distress of the sorrowful, the oppressed, the troubled, everywhere; the distress of captives in prison, of the suffering and the sick, of the forsaken, of the weak-minded in asylums, of those lying on operating tables in hospitals.

He sees all this, but at the same time He sees something else, something which we perhaps do not see, a need, a depth of misery which we in our blindness and shallowness do not see. He sees how all the need of the body and the soul, this unspeakable ruin of the glory of creation upon earth, becomes manifest in economic depression, in unemployment, in sickness, in the suffering and death of men. He sees that this is only the surface of a deeper need in the center of man's life. He lays hold of this hidden need, this unseen lash with which mankind is scourged; He marches upon it with the stride of a field marshal who enters battle to lay low his enemy. This is the misery upon which He fastens

His eyes, which He labels and attacks with the enigmatical word *sin, your sin.*

You come to me, He says, and your body is sick. Behold, there is something besides your body that is sick. You come to me and are caught, as in a prison, by the misery of your disease. Behold, you are confined in a dungeon entirely different from the bondage of your sickness. You want to be free. Yes, I understand you; but remember, fetters wholly different from those which you hold out to me must be broken; these will fall off when the other shackles with which you are bound are broken. You want to be healed—forgiveness is healing; "your sins"—I take them away! Behold, this is what He means by these words, thus are they to be understood, that Jesus forgives sin instead of healing sickness—no, not instead of healing, but when he forgives sins then He also heals disease.

We know, to some extent, what sin means. Sin means that you live in darkness; and the darkness is your guilt before Him who gave you life, who is your Lord, your God, and your Creator. I should like to point emphatically to the radical transformation of our way of thinking about these things that is effected through this story of Jesus. He puts the physical sufferings and bondage of man into the background and puts his spiritual suffering and captivity into the foreground. Who is not familiar with the external disorders of life!

War, sickness, nerves, hunger, poverty, failure,

bondage, distress of the time—all these together, seen
in the light of our text, are symptoms of a hidden, internal, disorder which has befallen us. Somehow, this
incident tells us, somehow it will break out in all of us,
as an illness breaks out from within, that *God* cannot be
with us, with His peace, His salvation, and His love, as
He really had designed to be.

Somehow, somewhere, it becomes evident in the body
of man, even in the body of each of us, that He cannot
be God as He desires to be. Why not? Because there is
an obstacle in the way, a barrier which towers mountain-
high between Him and us. This hindrance must be removed if life is to well up again into our disease. This
hindrance is called sin; and sin is laid hold of and overcome by the word *forgiveness*, forgiveness of sins.

In each one of us the question somehow has arisen:
Why does not God really help as He should help; why
is Christianity so weak and powerless? I am reminded
that modern youth asks these very questions, seeking
totally other powers of Christianity. They discover
again and again that the church remains debtor for the
answer. They have the right to ask.

I should say that the situation would be quite hopeless
if this question about the breaking forth of salvation and
truth among us were not asked. There is hope when this
question arises, though critically and iconoclastically,
perhaps in opposition to all Christian and churchly living. But there is real hope only when this question will
lead the questioners themselves, and with them our life,

to the one point at which the work within must begin if
God's salvation and help are really to come to us again.
This point of beginning, which concerns us and where
work must be done, is the forgiveness of sins.

One gets the impression, as one listens in to the God-
seeking of our day, that this search for God, this quest
after His help, misses the decisive point where God can
really be sought and found: the point which the Gospel
describes with the central words *sin* and *forgiveness*. You
seek God; you have the feeling that God is hidden from
you; thick walls separate you and your time from His
salvation and help. And you refer to this darkness, this
wall, when you speak of war, capitalism, industrial distress. This is true and yet it is not true. Behold, the
darkness, which gives birth to all other darknesses, is
guilt—your guilt, yours, man's guilt before God.

At this point you will find Jesus. Here He waits for
you with His decisive word. And if, perchance, with
your guilt you go unto Him and say, "My sins, my sins,
you must forgive them!"—then you have found *God*.
He has come to you, and thus salvation and help can
enter into your life. Why do we not always come to this
stopping-point—guilt and forgiveness? There is so
much longing in the world for release from all the needs
that may afflict us; but there is so little longing for deliverance from our sins in the sight of God.

Why do we not see this? Why do we not see the *need to*
come before God like the publican in the parable and cry
from afar, "God be merciful to me a sinner"? If men

were to come to this, then certainly the way would be open for help, yes, for salvation, to come directly into the crucial needs of our time.

If the merchant who has to do and must do with money; if the teacher, the tutor, who is and must be concerned with the imparting of spiritual values; if the individual in his interest and activities; if you and I, the merchant, the physician, the politician, the industrialist, also the shop girl, the maid, the father, the mother as governess—if they all can be brought to this point, where it will become plain to them that the external disorder of life is only the expression of an internal disorder with God, and that at the point within things must first be put into order and all external matters will right themselves, then we shall discover that if there is external disorder in our lives, difficulties of one's calling, problems of one's work, even material needs, and we let order be wrought within ourselves, then also the outer life will come into order; then ways will appear; then doors will open—I will not say wide doors and broad roads, but paths and gates by which we can go on our way.

The key is in the forgiveness of sins; for sin is the night and forgiveness is the key for the darkness: it is the light that transforms the central night, the night out of which all other nights come, and permits day to break.

Here it is in our story, so marvelously great yet so simple to read; Jesus has helped—has healed the body. Help flows out of the forgiveness of sins. Even when the body is sick and afflicted we can arise and walk. Why, then, is it so hard to permit ourselves to be led to this place, and there to be held fast?

Evidently, exceedingly much is required until the man, who we all are, comes to the point where he lays down his protests, his doubts, his deliberation, all his conceptions and ways of salvation with which he seeks to help himself, becomes poor and small, and can do nothing more than admit, "God, thou must help me and thou must so help me that thou wilt shatter my ego. I must admit that I am guilty before Thee. Take from me, take away from me, first, not what oppresses and distresses me; take my sin from me, then help has come to me." Then the old sovereignty falls, the tyranny over all of us of the idol *"I."*

He, this master in us, the "I," cannot and will not admit at any cost that he is guilty. The phrase "I am guilty" simply will not pass over the lips; this is apparent even in the small daily offenses between husband and wife; between parents and children; between fellows in work; and most certainly not in the major transactions of industry and politics. This *I* must be cast down. This idol *I* whom we serve falls when a man confesses his sins before God. And when man is shattered down to the roots, where sin is broken and the struggle for forgiveness takes place, then, in the light of history, some kind of turning and help occur.

This was the change that took place in the sixteenth century when Martin Luther, the obscure monk, was driven in his cloister to cry "My sins!" In this seeking and questing "how can I obtain a gracious God" he pressed on to the place where Jesus Christ our Saviour waits for us. And then for him there was light all the time.

That is the mystery of the message of the Bible—that here we are told of God whom we do not find in the glow of twilight, or in the blossoming tree that we admire, or in a creation of art, or even in the voice of conscience—no, not there; but we will find Him when we say to Him, "Thou creator of my life, I owe Thee everything; you must be merciful to me."

This is the message of the Bible: that here, in distinction from other gods which in the religions loom large before man, this GOD who is concerned about our life, yea, unspeakably concerned, comes before us and says: "O man that you are, if you depart ever so little from my commandments you are lost; and demons and devils gain the mastery over you and you are far from me." But this same God, who takes our sins so seriously, also gives grace, mercy, and forgiveness most freely; the God who sees you in your misery of body and soul and says to you: "Go thy way, you; your sins are forgiven!" Hold fast to this assurance and build your life upon it.

Why do we not see this? Why do we not see the supreme thing in the Bible: Jesus Christ appears with power before us and does for us the decisive work of life; lifts away the stone which lies on the road to God; takes upon Him the burden of sin and casts it aside; and the way is now open! Surely, through the wiles of the devil we are kept from seeing the closely related parts of this message: that he, ever and again, convinces us that our sins are harmless, and therefore we do not take seriously the forgiveness of sins. And we continue without help.

Just here is the problem and the work of the congregation of Jesus Christ. She shall help to confound the works and the wiles of the devil. Hers is the indescribably great task of surrounding the middle point of the Biblical message—the work of the Saviour—the forgiveness of sins—with her thoughts and words; to set to the fore this essence of the Bible and to magnify it before man so that it becomes clear that God is not far from any one of us; that we are sinners, but He is merciful, merciful without measure and without bound; that we may draw near and take out of His hand now, in our time, in our need, our specific need at this time—may draw out of His fullness grace for grace.

Let us not forget that Jesus Christ said to the paralytic not merely, "Thy sins are forgiven thee," but also, "Be of good cheer, my son." Yes, we also may be of good cheer, because the mystery of the work of the Saviour, the mystery of the power which is given Him upon earth, even to forgive sin, to cut fetters, to open prisons, to let help and light stream into this poor harassed world—the mystery of this might will shine among us and be magnified. May God grant that this come to pass; then we shall no longer need fear the course and outcome of these times and of our own life. Amen.

XVII.

JOY AND MODERATION

Rejoice in the Lord always: again I will say, Rejoice. Let your forbearance be known unto all men. The Lord is at hand.—Philemon 4:4-5.

When we rejoice, for some reason or perhaps for no reason, we approve our life, praise and love it as it is. If that is correct, when we rejoice and rejoice heartily we do so rightly. No one can really explain whence this self-rejoicing comes, for we do not always rejoice even though we have ever so many reasons for it, and oft-times our finest joy is without any reason at all. No one, therefore, can actually rouse us to rejoice. For when we do not rejoice it may be said that we simply cannot. Why, then, is some one to urge us to rejoice? "Rejoice for life . . . !" so one can sing to those only who already rejoice. Those who do not rejoice will hardly be moved to do so by such a song. They can only be counseled, as is done in that other "Song of Joy," "And he, who never could do so, let him steal weeping away from our midst!"

But the word "Rejoice," that we have just heard from Holy Writ, has nothing to do with the hymn "Re-

joice for Life." It does not take into consideration
whether we rejoice or do not rejoice. If, perchance, we
are joyful, the demands of the word are by no means
met; and if we should belong to those who cannot rejoice, we cannot be wooed and won by the question, "Do
we not have every reason for rejoicing? Is the fountain
of the finest, unfathomable joy choked up within us?"
Be that as it may, the command is "Rejoice!" That is to
say: Here it is not a matter of joy or no joy, nor a blend
of both, such as we may have brought into the church,
with which we may be filled when we look back upon
our past life or forward upon our future life, or when
we think upon this circumstance in life and that neighbor
of ours.

The word comes to us from without and confronts us
as a command: Rejoice! No one is excepted; not those
with light hearts and gay spirits, not those satisfied with
themselves and their lot, who one might think did not
need such an admonition—just they need it most of all.
Likewise not those whose hearts are heavy as lead,
whose eyes are filled with tears, who battle vainly day
and night with the demons of sadness, of whom one
might think, as they themselves probably think, that the
command "Rejoice!" was not meant for them—these
very persons, perhaps, can most readily hear and heed
the imperative "Rejoice!"

Be that as it may, here a bracket or a circle is drawn
around our existence or non-existence. Here, as in a
survey, everything is placed side by side—all that we

may experience as joy, whether fine or not so fine, higher or lower, sensuous, intellectual, or spiritual; also all joylessness, whether good or bad, serious or foolish. Here is also the deepest depth of our heart, from which ultimately and mysteriously all our joy or joylessness arises; only as a part of an inventory, one among others and contrary to all this, comes the command, wholly new and different, "Rejoice!"

Here all of life is brought into the picture. We are to rejoice not at this or that; although for each one something could be named for which one might rejoice. It is not said, "Rejoice in your heart," although in the heart of each one there is something for which one might and could rejoice. We are not told, "Rejoice in this beautiful season of Advent and Christmas," although it is a time when each one has cause for rejoicing. The command is simply: "Rejoice! Rejoice always!" That is, no matter when or where, no matter what our circumstances may be. Therefore we also are told so emphatically, "Rejoice! and again I say rejoice!" that no one may regard himself unchallenged or excluded, as if this rejoicing did not also concern him.

I tell you it concerns you, and directly you, who may be turning away either to the left or to the right. For we are commanded to rejoice in the name of Him to whom now belongs, and wholly belongs, your life and mine with all that we have and are, with all that has happened and that will happen. Not only because He is the eternal God, who created heaven and earth and all that

in them is, but because He took in the stable at Bethlehem— where there was much darkness and little light—
our human life and made it a part of His own life.

Further, because He always in this our human life,
dying on the cross, himself bore, and freed us from, all
the punishment which may and must afflict our lives.
And, finally, because—but always so that this our human
life is and remains His life—rising from the dead,
ascending into heaven, sitting on the right hand of God,
He is Lord over the most grievous sins and over the
whole reign of death in our life. In the name of this
Lord we are commanded, "Rejoice!" We are explicitly
told: "Rejoice in the Lord always!" He is the Lord
who has our life as His own life.

We need not inquire, therefore, whether we can or
cannot rejoice in His life as our own life. This question
is easily disposed of at the outset. Who can and dare
seriously say *Yes* to a life for whose depravity the Lord
could atone only on the cross? And who can and dare
say *No* to a life for whose justification He rose from the
dead? Is not the desire to praise and to love this life as
our own just as shortsighted as the contrary? Truly,
there clearly is an unconditioned and unlimited assent
to and rejoicing in life—without any admixture of dis-
sent; truly, there is an absolute loving and praising of
this our human life when we sing and say, "Blessed be
thou, Jesus Christ, that *thou* wast born man!" provided
we comprehend that this *thou* took our *I* to Himself,
yes, in His divine glory became our *I*.

Did not all the angels shout and sing praises "that thou becamest man?" And now shall this calculating man—to whom this matters, to whom God matters in this unheard of way, who continues a lengthy discussion —dare to take his joy or joylessness as a pretext not to rejoice in the Lord, or to rejoice not in the Lord but some other way? And now this calculating man is amazed when he is simply commanded, "Rejoice!"

Yes, what else remains for him? Christmas really means that nothing else remains for him. Christmas means that the ground upon which he thought he could live out his Yea and Nay, or his Nay and Yea, to his own life, has been taken from under his feet. Christmas means that His life—praise and thanks to God—is not, not any longer, his own life. But: "I shall praise the Lord forever; his praises shall always be in my mouth" (Ps. 34:1). For "this is my only comfort"—hear ye! my comfort and my only comfort—"in life and in death, that I with body and soul, both in life and in death, am not my own, but belong to my faithful Saviour, Jesus Christ." Therefore what is written avails for all, for all in every age: "Rejoice in the Lord always, and again I say, Rejoice!"

Is not the substance of what we are further told already clear? "Let your moderation be known to all men. The Lord is at hand." Is a law now given to us? Is this morality? Are we now to be told for the seventieth time that we are to be good, friendly, peaceful, brotherly, sisterly, to one another and to all men? Of course we need such admonitions, but we will be helped as little as when they were spoken to us many times before. No, only he can hear anything of law and morals who has not heard, or has forgotten, the decisive command, "Rejoice in the Lord!" Here is described in simplicity what takes place among those and through those who rejoice in the Lord; who hold fast to this and only to this, that the Word has become flesh.

Therefore we are explicitly told again, "The Lord is near," just as near as he was to those and as He is to us all, whose life He made His own, whose ground He has taken from beneath their feet, whose time is wholly in His hands. The meaning and substance of their life are *His* coming, *His* advent, the breaking in of *His* salvation. For "I will draw them all unto me" (John 12:32). His drawing of them is the meaning and substance of their life; also of *our* life, provided we are of those to whom the command, "Rejoice in the Lord!" has come with power. We are the servants who have to do only one thing, to watch and to wait for their Lord; Whom they—even when they have time, time to live, to work, their own time—know only as the Lord who is at hand, as the Lord who always speaks the saving word but also demands a reckoning from them. *We* are that! And therefore *we* are they of whom it is said, that to them, offering no resistance, something quite definite will happen.

The word which Luther translates "mildness" denotes, perhaps, conduct that is simple, fitting, seemly for men generally. And one perhaps cannot better describe this common trait—that which is fitting and seemly for those who rejoice in the Lord—than with the word "mildness." Luther rightly understood it when in his sermons on this text he emphasized ever and again that they who rejoice in the Lord are, as such, not in a position sincerely to claim a privilege over against their fellowmen. He liked to point to the words of Solomon, the preacher: "Be not righteous overmuch; neither make thyself overwise: why shouldst thou destroy thyself?" (Eccles. 7:16). And at one time he bluntly said: "Here Paul with one word annulled all rights."

Do we, perchance, think of the right which our good conscience or our better insight gives us, or of the right of the heart, which one person assumes he has or actually has as against another, or of the right of possession and of self-assertion? Certainly all these obtain. All these rights must and may be asserted at the proper place. But this place, the place where our own unredeemed human life takes a stand and claims its right—"The Lord is at hand," "I will draw all unto me"—is indeed attacked and besieged on all sides. It is threatened. It is seemly and fitting for us, who rejoice in the Lord, to assert and to defend our right here where we have it, not with the utmost confidence, but as those who in the end must surrender it.

The mastery over our life—praise and thanks be to God—is taken from us, and with it also the assumption that when we assert and defend our right we assert and

defend something true, real, eternal, divine. Nay! we
can use it only "as a shoemaker at work uses his needle,
awl, and thread, and lays them aside, or as a guest at the
inn uses food and couch only for temporal needs."

This, that is termed "mildness," is not so much demanded of us, but is described as the consequence of our
position. Our position is that of those "whose citizenship
is in heaven" (Phil. 3:20). But the consequence of this
position is this: that we conduct ourselves here only as
guests; that we play indeed earnestly with our right—
whatever its nature may be—but can only play. This
consequence is our sanctification. Our sanctification is
anything but a work to be thought and wrought by us.
It is an all-powerful award of the word of God. And
now it is said of this consequence—of our sanctification
—that it must be known to all men. Far be it that for
this we have to do something special.

Humbled beneath the severity and the goodness of
God, we need be only what we are. Whether we are this
will be decided finally if the consequence is drawn and
becomes visible. It is indeed true that without joy in the
Lord we shall doubtless continue the old stubbornness
of opinion of each against all; continue that deadly seriousness with which the so-called good, even more than
the so-called wicked, make life bitter for one another
and turn this world into a hell; continue the annihilating
war carried on by both sides consciously or unconsciously
in the name of the ideal, often of the Christian ideal.

How can moderation be in us and be made known

through us unless we hold that the Word became flesh; that Jesus Christ took our life to Himself; and that He is actually our life and is surety for us? Without justification, no sanctification.

The reverse is also true: Where there is no visible sanctification there is no justification. The matter stands thus: we can remain unmoved, seated on the thrones of our right as open or secret kings, where the surly, sad quarrels about the alleged divine claims which we hold against one another can continue as if nothing had happened, as if only a little bit of Christianity and theology had been added, to make us all the more secure—how can there be joy in the Lord? Here, it is generally known, that is not sought which is above, where Christ sitteth on the right hand of God. Furthermore, it is not believed that the Word became flesh.

Because we are not now in the dark world of law and morals but in the world of God, one thing fits into the other with uncanny precision. Your moderation *must* become known to all men. If it does not become known, then it is not here; and were it not here, then you would by no means be what you are, children of your Father reconciled in Christ Jesus. But you are this, and therefore your moderation is here, and, as the city which is upon a hill cannot be hid, your moderation must become known to all men.

Christmas must come among men. People, all people, wait for the time when they may rejoice. Even with all their bitter, despairing joylessness, they prove how eagerly they desire to rejoice. But how can they really rejoice as they would like to rejoice for their own life, after Jesus Christ was born for them, and was crucified and risen, and thereby has already taken their life whether they know it or not?

In the utter absence of comfort for the lack of that which the so-called Christmas season brings into our public life and into our homes in the dreadful admixture of open caricature and secret sadness, do we not clearly understand that man, in his endeavor to rejoice in his own life, lives and moves only in the gray twilight of a joy not wholly sincere, and—let us say it openly—of a joylessness not wholly sincere? Why? Because such a distinctive life for man, in which and in which alone he really can rejoice, is to be had at no other place and in no other way than in the Lord at the right hand of God. And now let me ask: What else can man hope for than that some time he may truly rejoice? How else could Christmas come among men than that they hear how this happened and happens? But how can they hear if it be not made known?

And now let us not be so naïve or so indolent as to think that it is sufficiently made known when it is preached here and there in churches. Oh that it were preached in all churches with the utmost decision! Would that our Evangelical Church would again become a place where on Christmas and on each Sunday of the year this one thing were proclaimed and heard unceasingly, "The Word became flesh; therefore rejoice in the Lord always." But Sunday is only one of seven days in the week. And by sermons alone the church cannot proclaim the word of God, which it is her mission to proclaim.

Many people can no longer, or not yet, understand sermons. If by chance the persons who yesterday cried out in our streets, "We are hungry," were today in church, it is evident that they could not understand that here glad tidings are proclaimed for them also. And who would arraign them on that account? This is so not for the first time at present. For the Apostle Paul not only preached in public but he besought the congregation, "Let your moderation be known to all men."

Your sanctification is the other necessary proclamation. Did not Jesus Christ Himself say "Let your light so shine before men that they may see your good works and glorify your father which is in heaven"? Let us not imagine that for the sake of our personal salvation we are sanctified and bearers of light. Nor are we called to love and to praise our life in Christ, hidden in God, for the sake of our personal salvation. But we are this, and are to do this, for the sake of the service which God wants from us. This we are to His honor; this we are for the purpose of this other proclamation.

And precisely for this other proclamation people wait —all people—as truly as Jesus Christ was born, died, and rose for all. On no account believe that they wait for the distribution of Christmas presents. These may and also must be given; and your moderation will also be known in this, that you consider and then act accordingly; that, only in play and by no means in earnest, the one can be better situated beside so many more poorly situated, and therefore cannot keep his purse under lock and key. But what they really wait for is your moderation itself; persons whose confidence in their own right is so shattered that they can only half-heartedly fight for their right; persons who no longer with the aid of ideas and ideals harden themselves toward one another; persons who know that they can be right only when they are wrong; persons who not by their own insight and efforts but by decree of the Omnipotent have been brought to the point where they bow not only before God but (as an evidence that they do so before God) before every man in his sinfulness and misery.

Depend on this: Your moderation will speak there where many a sermon will not be heard. It will speak not of your virtues but of the virtues of Him who has called us into His wonderful light; not of your sanctification but of the justification of sinners through God's free grace; not of the glory and wealth of Christianity but of the glory of Jesus Christ, who came to seek and to save that which was lost. Your moderation, because it is nothing other than common humanity, and yet in its humility is uncommon humanity, will testify to your joy in the Lord which shall be to all people. Go forth and proclaim to them this word, which can be spoken only by deed, the unpretentious deed, of free lords who at any moment may become servants.

I know what you wish to ask. You want to ask the doubtful question whether they, then, whether indeed all men—your neighbors, of whom each one of you may now be thinking—will hear the word; whether there will not also be unbelief and stubbornness.

Yes, that will be so. But what is that to us? It is not in our power to convert one another by either preaching or doing the word. What then is in our power? We can only hear what we are and what follows because of what we are. Jesus Christ took the unbelief of men seriously because He did not take it seriously. If our unbelief were a serious matter to him, if it appeared to Him as an obstacle, who of us then could presume to be His? To believe in Him is to believe always that He is greater than our sins. But how can we go on our way in this faith and take seriously the sin and unbelief of our fellowmen?

Faith must always mean that in sincerity and without wavering we do not believe in the unbelief of others; that we never wish to be relieved from serving them; and that we shall not let them go, as Jesus Christ does not let us go despite our unbelief. Let us go to them in the Christmas spirit with the assurance that we can and shall know nothing else than this, that through God's incomprehensible miracle we have a Lord who has shown us mercy—mark well!—mercy.

XVIII.

THE GLORY OF JESUS

And the third day there was a marriage in Cana of Galilee; and the mother of Jesus was there: and Jesus also was bidden, and his disciples, to the marriage. And when the wine failed, the mother of Jesus saith unto him, They have no wine. And Jesus saith unto her, Woman, what have I to do with thee? mine hour is not yet come. His mother saith unto the servants, Whatsoever he saith unto you, do it. Now there were six waterpots of stone set there after the Jews' manner of purifying, containing two or three firkins apiece. Jesus saith unto them, Fill the waterpots with water. And they filled them up to the brim. And he saith unto them, Draw out now, and bear unto the ruler of the feast. And they bare it. And when the ruler of the feast tasted the water now become wine, and knew not whence it was (but the servants that had drawn the water knew), the ruler of the feast calleth the bridegroom, and saith unto him, Every man setteth on first the good wine; and when men have drunk freely, then that which is worse: thou hast kept the good wine until now. This beginning of his signs did Jesus in Cana of Galilee, and manifested his glory; and his disciples believed on him.—*John 2:1-11.*

In this story—as incomprehensibly great as it is enigmatical and mysterious—precisely that is unimportant which often claims our first attention. It is not important that the miracle at Cana was wrought at a wedding. It is not important that the guests were served with wine

made of water. In the church far too large a place in
the interpretation of this event has been given to the
wedding and the wine. Men have tried to show that
Jesus desired to give joy to a bridal pair on their wedding
day and with his gift to bless the marriage. Painters
have portrayed Jesus as a pastor blessing bride and
groom.

At the same time others, opponents of alcoholic
liquors, took offense because Jesus made wine for the
bridal party, taking it for granted that He was opposed
to the use of alcohol as a beverage. And again others
believed that by this act of Jesus they could justify
sumptuous feasting. With all this the incident has
nothing in the least to do. What was the purpose of
Jesus? This is stated plainly at the end of the story:
"He manifested his glory." That was His purpose,
that was the important thing, the end in view; and upon
that we must persistently fix our thoughts.

The thing of importance is not the wedding feast, but
that something occurred at the wedding feast. Mary
said to him, "They have no wine." In other words, an
embarrassing situation, a want, a distress—if we care to
call it that—was at hand. In the midst of the festivities
something gave out that seemed to be indispensable for
the continuance of the festal joy. At all events the
wedding guests felt that way; and Mary only said what
they all thought: If the wine stops flowing, then the
feasting and the celebrating and the gayety are at an
end.

It appears, does it not, that an incidental, small, almost vulgar, perplexing situation is here depicted for us. Is there nothing worse than a wedding feast at which the wine is about to fail? We might say that the worst of all the disagreeable and awkward situations which make up our days are these: a walk spoiled by rain, a mislaid key, a missed train; or perhaps a little toothache, or a hat blown away by the wind.

How can we regard these things as important? But observe, it is only another way of saying: Yes, you may look into life where you will—wherever men have to live—and you will find something which causes men to sigh, to complain, to falter, and to worry. And perhaps to the very persons who are now at this place these embarrassments appear not at all unimportant. They are spoken of long afterward. Perhaps we may go still farther and say that if one looks upon life from afar, then perhaps the so-called great and greatest perplexities appear unimportant and quite incidental. Perchance we may hear of a person, who does not concern us, that he was sick and has recovered.

How trivial this affair appears because it does not concern us! And the sufferings of whole ages and nations, if only they are far enough in the past—how little they affect us! In the final analysis, what is small and what is great? The world seen from the sun is an anthill; and the things that happen there, of what significance are they?

Now the outstanding thing told us is that Jesus is in

the midst of these small and great perplexities, needs, and anxieties. He was there when the wine gave out; and his mother told him about it. What does He do? He says, "Woman, what have I to do with thee?" What does this mean? Does it mean something different from what has just been said? "What have I to do with these trifles? Do not bother me with them. I have nothing to do with them." To be sure, that is the first meaning of this answer. Countless things are to him insignificant which to us seem important. But that is not all: something more, entirely different, is hidden in this answer. For we are told how Jesus took up this quite minor, incidental, trifling matter, this bagatelle; how he felt himself constrained to make wine out of water; how, through this small need, he threw into the balance the last and greatest, all the power and glory bestowed upon him.

Then, at all events, the want is met and wine is served in abundance to the guests. Yes, the non-essential thing is important enough to cause him to do that which is supremely great—"to manifest his glory." Just that: HIS GLORY! Not the wine, which now stands on the table before the guests, but He, He Himself, Jesus, who stands before them whose eyes are now opened to see his glory—this is the important thing; upon this everything depends, and around this everything turns.

Quite a small question, a mere trifle, is brought to Jesus. But his answer is immeasurably great. As if a thimbleful of need had been held out to him and he knew how to put an ocean of help before those who brought to him an infinitesimal need.

What is this to signify? Come, let us again think of all the little needs, perplexities, sorrows, and cares of which our lives consist: the misplaced keys, the lost book, headache, anxiety of love, perchance also your illness, the death in your family, the secret need that has come upon you. Indeed, all of us are in want of something somewhere, every day, every hour. There is always something amiss, distasteful, irritating, interrupting our joy. Life, in reality, is a thing replete with needs; and we can understand the perplexity of the wedding guests at Cana. But the story tells us one thing in the midst of the flood of the perplexities of life: it tells us that your need is not at all in that which you suffer; but your need is at an entirely different place. It is true, indeed, that the little annoyances of life, even though we suffer so much, are really *little* annoyances.

However, the deep need and perplexity of life, which probably we do not at all see, are to be found in an entirely different place. Behind all the great and small, the small and great, problems of life, as they may be termed, in the depths, in the background of our being, something colossal is burning. All the small anxieties, all the great and small perplexities of life, are here only that we may be mindful of this deep, great, last, burning need of life. There is scarcely a word great and comprehensive enough to include and express this last, deepest perplexity of life. The greatest word in our language for the greatest being is the word "God." This is just the right word to tell us where our need is. Not the mislaid key, not the toothache, not your illness, nor your sorrows though considerable—all this is not the source of your trouble. But GOD is lacking; and because God is lacking all is lacking. Because God is wanting, life is so much in need. Because the great, the last, is not in order, therefore, the little and the least also are not in order.

Observe, one may liken the thousand perplexities of life to the specially dark places through which we may have to pass in a night's journey. But, at all events, one is able to help one's self by lighting candles, which give a little light at the darkest places. But all these lights cannot do one thing: they cannot turn night into day; and therefore it remains dark despite all the secondary helps which we can provide for ourselves. Jesus, however, in the midst of the perplexities of life, is not concerned merely with the removal of these minor distresses.

"What is it to me that your wine is failing? What is it to me that your life appears broken here and there?" His work is this: to change the whole need of life. His purpose is not to light up the night; he would change the night into day. That is his work. For that he was commissioned when he came into the world. This is what is here called "his glory." This is his glory, that he does not give aid here and there, but that he transforms the whole life by bringing God and man together again.

And now let it be said unto us in the midst of the many perplexities of life which will surround us as soon as we are again on the outside, today, tomorrow, and the day after tomorrow; let it be said to us in the midst of the little personal needs and anxieties from which we suffer; let it be said in the great crises of our day, which will seem small to a later generation; let it be said to us that where we suppose something is wrong with you and me nothing at all is wrong. We are in need of something entirely different. We do not have the greatest of all; we are without God and His help. We do not have the revelation of the glory of Jesus. That alone can help us in our need whether great or small.

Yes, you cannot really comfort a child and direct him to the right path without knowledge of Him who only is great, of the help and the power of the living God. You cannot take up even the smallest problem of life and solve it without knowing the glory of Him through whom you live. One will find the great in the smallest and the whole in the part. That, indeed, means that we must take the small and the smallest so seriously that, even in the small and the smallest matter, the greatest denial and the greatest need, and therefore, also, the greatest help, can come to us as a brightly burning light.

It was always so where the glory of Jesus came as

help to men in need; some complaint, a casual need,
something about to fail, was taken seriously by a person.
Then the great light shone into these small affairs. Was
it not an immeasurably small, trifling, incidental occasion, when in the year 1505-1520 the obscure monk
Martin Luther in his cloister was compelled to take
seriously his personal needs even unto blood? What
did that signify in the sixteenth century from the standpoint of the history of mankind? Did Luther mean
anything beside the great princes and emperors—this
monk, wrestling with a question and a need, of which
his confessor said: "Stop worrying; these are baby
sins"? But he could not stop. He took a small matter
seriously and in it he found the greatest of all.

Was it not something insignificant from the standpoint of the history of the world that, in the beginning
of the nineteenth century, in a forgotten village in the
Swabian Jura, Blumhardt, a country pastor, met an
hysterical maiden and took seriously her illness, in which
the issue of life as a whole was involved? Through
this small incident the great glory of Jesus was manifested.

The glory of Jesus, what is it? Let me say only one
thing: We are all baptized into the name of Jesus. In
the first days and weeks of life the seal of this name was
put upon us. Clearly we did not at the time comprehend the meaning of this act. Perhaps we do not even
now understand it. For innumerable persons throughout life baptism has no special import. What does it

mean? It means that, from infancy, men and women cannot go through life without the glory and the help contained in the name of Jesus. What are the glory and help of Jesus?

Here we must turn our eyes away from everything and look in an entirely different direction; or, I might more truthfully say, we must close our eyes and listen to something that is told us: that beyond this world and time, beyond all trouble and confusion in which we live our little life, which we must always regard as infinitely important—beyond this is the real important event for us, God, the Eternal, who made heaven and earth; the holy and living God, the mysterious and hidden One, whom we cannot conceive with our sinful minds, of whom we of ourselves know nothing; He, full of mystery, concealed, eternal, living, has done something for us; He has turned toward us. Yes, a turning from heaven to earth, from God to man, has taken place. God, God Himself, came out of Himself and came down into this anthill of the world's history, into this infinitely small and paltry world. He humbled himself at a certain time and place and took the form of a man. Where Jesus, his life, is, there is the place full of mystery. And all this, because he would meet us. God would meet you, would meet me.

You may meet Him, the Eternal, the Holy One, the Merciful One; this is the message of the Bible; for this Jesus Christ came into the world. This is the glory of the Son who stands before us at Cana. And now Jesus lives in the form of man among us, so that we can meet Him and really apprehend Him and realize that we are in his hands, that He is merciful and gracious beyond measure. This is the matter at stake. All the needs of life flow together into this one need of the secrecy of God; and all the help of life wells forth like a stream of living water from this one spring, the Son who comes unto us and shows us the glory of the Father, that glory which consists in nothing else than the power with which the Father, God Himself, would enter our little human life in order to say to us: "You little perverse child, you are dear to me; you are my child; I have redeemed you; you will remain mine and nothing shall take you out of my hands." To permit that to be said to us, that is faith.

Something infinitely little happened at the wedding at Cana. Into the midst of the infinitely little things of life came an embarrassment, a need. Jesus met it; there is wine on the table, the feast can go on. Neither the wine nor the continuance of the feast is of importance; but that this wine, this approach to man, becomes a symbol of the mercy and nearness of God, of the new day, the day of salvation and of help, that has dawned upon the confusion of the world's life. Do we also have such signs? Yes, in our present needs God's word is given us.

We have also for a sign something human, a book of events and words; but this book and these events and these words are evidence of the glory of the Son who brings us the Father. And God has given us something more tangible, above and beyond the word: He has set for us the table with bread and wine as at Cana.

This bread and this wine on the Lord's table are nothing more than appropriate symbols by which when you take them you are told: "God lives; I am his child; He keeps me, and all time, and the world with its thousand perplexities and problems, in his merciful hand." Do you not suppose that this, if we let it be told us, will cling to us; that it will remain fastened in us; that it will really call us in our dreams? Do you not believe that we shall then go, with a different spirit and mood, on our way with our great and small perplexities and needs? Come forth, thou small confused child of man; be a courageous child of God, for your Saviour says, "I am thy good shepherd." Amen.

THE END